The Stranglers
LA FOLIE

In-depth

Laura Shenton

The Stranglers
LA FOLIE

In-depth

Laura Shenton

WYMER
PUBLISHING
Bedford, England

First published in 2022 by Wymer Publishing
Bedford, England www.wymerpublishing.co.uk Tel: 01234 326691
Wymer Publishing is a trading name of Wymer (UK) Ltd

Copyright © 2022 Laura Shenton / Wymer Publishing. This edition published 2022.

Print edition (fully illustrated): **ISBN: 978-1-912782-02-8**

Edited by Jerry Bloom.

eBook formatting by Coinlea.

A catalogue record for this book is available from the British Library.

Typeset by Andy Bishop / 1016 Sarpsborg
Cover design by 1016 Sarpsborg.
Cover photo and all other group photos © Alan Perry Concert Photography.

Contents

"I believe everyone has had a close contact with madness, an encounter of the first kind, but one can, equally, taste the third kind. I believe many people have experienced this at one stage or another. I myself have experienced it, about a year ago during the Meninblack period. Three of us, for that matter, have shared that kind of encounter, during the last three years. Separately, but definitely linked to the Meninblack."

Jean-Jacques Burnel, 1981

"The Stranglers have surprised everyone with their lyrical offering, 'Golden Brown'."

The Daily Mirror, 1982

Preface

By November 1981 when *La Folie* was released, a lot had happened to The Stranglers since the successes of 1977. Due to the band's changes in musical direction and the difference in the landscape of popular music overall, the way in which the music press — and their fans — related to the group had inevitably changed. Punk and rock was largely overshadowed by the popularity of synthesiser-dominated pop and the new romantics (and of course, drum machines!).

Even in comparison to two-tone music from the likes of Madness and The Specials, The Stranglers seemed old-fashioned to many. Not only that, but The Stranglers' brushes with the law had arguably got a lot more serious. Of course, to try and rigidly categorise The Stranglers as punk is not the ideal but as far as the music press were concerned, in 1980 and the earlier part of 1981, The Stranglers made weird music and were always in trouble. Overall, things were not looking good. Vitally, this is essential context for being able to look at *La Folie* objectively in terms of what the album did for The Stranglers' career at a time when really, things could have gone either way for them.

As author of this book, it's only right to be transparent and to state that I think *La Folie* is a fantastic album. I don't think there's a bad track on it. I promise though — I *absolutely promise!* — to be objective in my commentary of the album. In order to do this, I will refer to a range of sources that include many vintage reviews and interviews. I don't want the narrative of this book to be centred on my own bias. So yes, whilst I'm writing this book as someone who thinks *La Folie* is brilliant, a lot of the content will be from sources that enable me to present the most balanced narrative possible.

As I mentioned in my other book, *The Stranglers 1977*, I have no affiliation with The Stranglers or with any of their associates. I have no bias in that regard and besides that, this book is a gossip-free zone anyway. I want to present how the music resonated with people at the time and not what my perception of it is as one of millions of fans out there.

Chapter One

Why La Folie?

In November 1981, just nine months after the release of *The Gospel According To The Meninblack*, The Stranglers released *La Folie*. The period in between the release of those two albums was an incredibly turbulent one for the band.

The Gospel According To The Meninblack was their first album to sell less than 50,000 copies after a good few months of being released. The drop in sales was such that it prompted EMI to question whether The Stranglers would be worth investing in further. The last Stranglers single to have got within the top ten was 'No More Heroes' in 1977. Complexly, although the *Meninblack* album had got to number eight upon its release, it dropped off from the top forty very quickly thereafter. A lack of commercial songs on it was probably a key factor.

When the *Meninblack* album was due out, Hugh Cornwell told *Sounds* in January 1981; "It's not just a collection of songs. It's very moody music and a lot of it's very spacey and more varied in style. You can't really talk about your music… This album is the first one where all the tracks have a cohesion about them. They're all dealing with strange phenomena."

Dave Greenfield said; "And alternative ways of looking at religions through these extraterrestrial phenomena. The nearest we've done to a concept album."

Cornwell elaborated; "We're not the Meninblack. The Meninblack are a phenomenon that occurs all over the world, people seeing UFOs and sighting strange phenomena and getting visited by men wearing black suits and hats and open-toed sandals and drive around in fifties cars and enter people's houses and speak to them and after half an hour or so they leave again and they put these people into trances with thought implantation or whatever."

Greenfield continued: "Hypnosis. They impart information that if the people are saying too much about what they've seen, they won't say anything anymore."

Cornwell: "There's been lots of reports in the journals all over the world. They're sort of close encounters really. These guys have no facial hair and they sort of resemble human beings but aren't the bona fide thing. These people never see flying saucers again, or they die or disappear afterwards or strange things happen to them. It is a strange occurrence."

The Stranglers' prior album, *The Raven*, had also not been the most accessible for listeners. With that too having limited appeal to a wider audience, after the *Meninblack* album, it was clear that something more commercial was needed.

Whilst The Stranglers took this into account, with *La Folie*, they still managed to make an end product that was very much their own. Now, the album itself got to number eleven but in getting to number two, the single of 'Golden Brown' would do amazing things for them. Luckily for the band, the single made an impact that would show how accessible The Stranglers' music could be. It was a vital achievement considering that their last two best-charting singles had been 'No More Heroes' and prior to that, 'Peaches' which had both peaked at number eight.

"Suddenly it all turned around again very quickly with 'Golden Brown'," said Jet Black. "Things tend to do that in rock 'n' roll — you're up one minute, down the next. Did we take risks? Well, I mean, the whole thing's a risk. You get no guarantees in this game."

Speaking to MTV in 1990, Cornwell said; "We were very down. That record got the LP to go around. It was our last chance with that record company. And luckily, it cracked through."

La Folie went where other Stranglers albums hadn't. It deals with ideas and emotions that hadn't been touched upon in their previous work. Not only that, but Hugh Cornwell's vocals moved to a more gentle and melancholic sound. Whether the themes on the album were being dealt with sincerely or ironically is subject to discussion of course, but still.

Due to the way in which *La Folie* was so different to any of The Stranglers' previous albums, for many of their fans who had supported them from the early days, there was a sense of disillusion; *how could the band have made such a departure from the hard, aggressive sounds of 1977 that had so often seen them lumped in with the likes of the Sex Pistols and The Damned?!* After all, carrying a hit like 'Golden Brown', *La Folie* was nothing like the pub rock moments on *Rattus Norvegicus* and *No More Heroes*. Additionally, the move away from the experimental style on *The Meninblack* signified that The Stranglers were going in a new direction with *La Folie*.

French fanzine *Black & White* put it to Jean-Jacques Burnel in 1982; "Compared with *Meninblack*, the sound of your guitar on this LP seems to go back to a more traditional basis. It also sounds less predominant and disassociated, giving more integrity and force to your music. Do you share this opinion?" His response: "Yes, absolutely. Well said. Nothing to add."

Much like *Meninblack* though, *La Folie* is arguably a loose concept album in how each number is centred on various ideas about love. On the opening track, 'Non Stop', it is difficult to tell whether Cornwell is singing the words cheerfully, sarcastically, or perhaps a little of both as he speaks of a nun who "claims she waited her life for a man" and "says she's not frustrated in any way."

Burnel said in 1990, "The first two albums were similar. They were done in the same session. Every album since then was quite drastically different. Whether it was from a song point of view or because of just the technology we were using."

It would be a mistake to consider that the manic energy that The Stranglers brought to the table on previous albums is absent from *La Folie*. Cornwell's vocals on 'Let Me Introduce You To The Family' are done with force. Backed by Jet Black's staccato drumming and a guitar line abundant in distortion, there is certainly no lack of passion on *La Folie*. In fact, every track on the album is played with strength, whether it be the glass-half-empty mood on 'How To Find True Love And Happiness In The Present Day' or the upbeat rock of 'Pin Up'. As romantic as it sounds overall, even Dave Greenfield's harpsichord line on 'Golden Brown' is played in a way that is driving (probably vital considering the complex use of time signature! More on that later).

With *La Folie*, did The Stranglers go *that* far away from their original sound though? Considering a track like 'Everybody Loves You When You're Dead' — with its subversive lyrics and simple guitar and bass lines — it becomes clear that still, The Stranglers' music didn't lose all of the qualities that had inspired people to compare their music to punk.

Of course, the punk label that many chose to put on The Stranglers had been a point of debate since the band's early days. With punters spitting at gigs to songs that many argued contained angry and chauvinist lyrics, it's easy to see how it happened. Whether or not anyone — or indeed The Stranglers themselves — agreed with the punk label, there's no getting past the fact that sometimes the band were able to play on this to their advantage in terms of getting promotional press coverage whilst equally sometimes feeling that the label did a disservice to the complexity of their music (for instance, since when did the Sex Pistols think to use a keyboard?).

Even in 1977, some insisted that The Stranglers were too old to be punk. After all, Jet Black was just shy of forty years old around that time. It was also the case that many in the punk crowd regarded The Stranglers' musical ability and execution to be excessive. Either way, being lumped in with punk in the late seventies was advantageous to The Stranglers overall. They arrived on the scene when the aim was to get regular pub gigs around London and hey, the crowds were up for it so why not?

Cornwell told *Melody Maker* in February 1990; "The idea that punk swept away all the old dinosaur bands was a romantic thing for the history books. Punk was thought up by about four people: Malcolm McLaren, Dai Davies, Andrew Logan the artist and Bernie Rhodes. They all sat around for a couple of evenings in the mid-seventies and thought, 'Sod all this, let's create something!' And that was it! All that stuff about the voice of rebellion was a load of rubbish. It was a scam, and luckily it was so original it got its own life."

In joking that the whole punk thing was perhaps something of a scam, he added; "I didn't know exactly what scam was going on. I wasn't sure what it was, but the fact that it had record companies jumping round like they were on hot coals… I'm not stupid, I knew that for them all to be caught with their pants down, there was a spectacular scam going on. They're scammers themselves, so it had to be a very clever one." When asked if he found punk "funny to look back on?" Cornwell said; "Oh, it is. Very funny. Very, very funny."

When asked to what extent he considered The Stranglers to be part of the punk movement, Burnel told *Black & White* in 1982; "I've always felt a part of it to a certain extent. I was the only one of The Stranglers to think that way though. No, in fact it was kind of a mutual benefit to society. We eased the position in England, as we already had our own following. But at the same time, it meant that people were ready to welcome us. A favourable time for The Stranglers. There were also lots of points in common. We've always had violence, extremism, tight trousers, short hair. Even ideologically, on a controversial level, but not musically. Everyone used to say, 'There's no need for keyboards and synths.' In short, we were the first to use a synth and did so even on the first album. Purists were shocked. We don't give a damn!"

Overall, by 1981, with an album like *La Folie* following the *Meninblack* one, The Stranglers' career had reached a point where it was less frequent for them to be lumped in with punk and were, thanks to 'Golden Brown', seen as a band who could stand alongside any other successful synth pop band that was going strong at the time (synth pop was huge around that time with The Human League's *Dare* album gracing the charts around the same time as *La Folie*'s release).

It is impressive that whilst The Stranglers were able to make the most of the punk label during their early days, five years later, they were able to emerge as something different without selling out completely. *La Folie* is just as intelligent, well-executed and original as anything The Stranglers had done previously, it's just that the album was that much more accessible that it would open new commercial doors for the band.

After the success of *Rattus Norvegicus* and *No More Heroes* in 1977 and then *Black And White* in 1978, The Stranglers parted ways with Martin Rushent as producer. Cornwell said in 1979; "We're never going to use a producer again. They are just shitty little parasites. All they're good for is telling jokes. And we know better jokes than any of 'em."

Burnel said in later years "He just said, 'I can't be doing with this' and walked out. We just carried on. We were kids in a candy store. It was the start of digital technology and we had a keyboard player who could outplay anyone. Fantastic."

In October 1984, Cornwell told *Smash Hits*; "We ended up feeling quite righteous because, on the one hand, we were rejecting what had come before, but everything that was new was rejecting us. So, obviously, we ended up a little belligerent."

Of The Stranglers' early days, Burnel told *New Musical Express* in February 1990; "We were the hardest. Nobody was harder than us. It seemed to matter at the time. It got stupid though, it got to the stage where I couldn't walk down the street. I knew it was time to get out of London when I walked down a market street and three traders tried to pick a fight with me one after the other." Cornwell added: "You are the victim of an image."

When asked if they believed their own hype in the early days of the band, Jet Black told *New Musical Express* in February 1990; "At times I think we did. I mean all that stuff about racing across the Queensland border chased by secret police in helicopters firing at us was all made up by some journalist but we never denied it because it was fun. But I *did* put a table through a plate glass window once — I was drunk and was really frustrated having spent three days in Spain and everything was closed. That left me with this thug image for life. Actually I don't mind being seen as a thug because actually it has its finer moments."

In 1979, The Stranglers were advised by their management to break up. It was felt by them that the band had lost direction. Dismissing this idea, the band parted ways with their management team. It saw Burnel releasing an experimental solo album, *Euroman Cometh*, backed by a small UK tour. Cornwell released the album *Nosferatu* in collaboration with Robert Williams — at the time, drummer with Captain Beefheart. Also that year, The Stranglers released *The Raven*. It signified a transition towards a more melodic and complex sound which appealed more to the album than the singles market. In such regard the approach the band had taken to the album was different to that which had been encouraged by Martin Rushent.

The Raven is a thematically diverse album in how it deals with a range of subjects: a Viking's lonely voyage, heroin addiction, genetic engineering and political occurrences of the day. And of course, the extraterrestrial visitors the Meninblack. *The Raven*, really, was the first Stranglers album to demonstrate a departure from the distinctive sound of the band's earlier three albums. *The Raven* didn't see a US release until six years after it had been released elsewhere, but it did well in the UK where it got to number four. It also featured the singles 'Duchess' (which got to number fourteen), 'Nuclear Device' (which got to number thirty-six) and 'Don't Bring Harry' (which got to number forty-one).

In total, The Stranglers' first four albums had done well enough that by the time it came to making the fifth one, the band were given complete freedom. This is how *The Gospel According To The Meninblack* came to be. As a concept album, the theme was a bold one that explored religion and the way that it supposedly connected with religious phenomena and extraterrestrial visitors. The album was far from anything that The Stranglers had done before and consequently it alienated a lot of their fans (no pun intended, genuinely!). Peaking at number eight, it was the lowest chart position for a Stranglers album at the time. Realistically, this wasn't the end of the world but it certainly signified that based on the musical and thematic obscurity of the album, The Stranglers were in a place of uncertainty on what to do next.

It wasn't just musically that things were up in the air in the early eighties prior to the release of *La Folie*. (And that isn't to say that everything was going terribly before *La Folie* and that from that album onwards everything was perfect; it's just that when looking at some of the things The Stranglers went through in 1980 and early 1981, it's amazing that they managed to keep going at all!).

Just before the release of *La Folie* though, it was very much the case that The Stranglers' antics outside of the music itself would see them make the headlines for many challenging reasons. It must have been frustrating for a band who probably just wanted to get on with the music more than anything. Cornwell told *Sounds* in January 1981; "It's just that people always took us the wrong way... We just get misinterpreted. Maybe we just don't speak plain English enough or something."

Jet Black told the *Liverpool Echo* in October 1981; "It used to appeal to my wicked sense of humour to see the way people used to react to us. All this mean, moody macho stuff — a load of cobblers old chap. Cobblers! As I have said, I think we must be the most misunderstood band in the world. There are some — a gifted minority who see through our guises — they understand the humour. The others take it on its face value. That's where the confrontation starts and ends. Once you are put in a category by the music business its like being put in our own coffin. There's no way out."

Burnel told *Black & White* in 1982; "I believe, in fact, that on the contrary we have a lot more humour than most. I don't see anything depressing in the subjects we approach whether it be the colour black, or death. No, it must be that our humour is too subtle or clever for them!"

Cornwell told the BBC in 1982; "It's a bit sad picking up something about yourselves and all you read is about that band that is famous for doing that and that and it doesn't say that band are famous for making good music. And that's why we're doing it really; we're not playing in a band to have stories saying we're bad boys written about us. It's silly. We're doing it because we write music and we'd like to be appreciated for writing good music. So whenever we are associated in the press for doing nothing to do with music, it's a bit depressing."

Understandably though, some stories were just too sensational for the press to ignore. *Record Mirror* reported in January 1980; "Stranglers' Hugh Cornwell was given an eight-week prison sentence and fined £300 at the West London Court on Monday, when he admitted to five charges of possessing drugs — including cannabis, heroin and cocaine. Also charged was rock promoter Paul Loasby, who works for Harvey Goldsmith Entertainments. Loasby admitted one charge of possessing drugs and was given a fourteen-day sentence. Both Cornwell and Loasby have appealed against their sentences and were given unconditional bail. The police say they stopped the pair at a "routine roadblock" at London's Hammersmith Broadway on November 1st last year and found drugs in the car."

"Magistrate Eric Crowther said: 'You are two intellectual men of mature years who have a great influence on the lifestyle of teenagers and who should not cause damage to the morals and physical wellbeing of those who admire you. Both of you have a university education which makes your involvement in the drug scene all the more contemptible. You have deliberately chosen to flaunt the law.' The defence told the court that Cornwell, thirty, was a science graduate who had given up a promising career in medical research to form his band in 1974. If the conviction stands, there could be problems about the Stranglers' future dates abroad as both the States and Japan are known to take a tough line with visitors who have been convicted for any drug offence. A concert tour of India, Thailand and Australia has already been cancelled."

Vitally, despite the fact that Cornwell was indeed put behind bars, the rest of The Stranglers — and other artists — were in full support of him. *Record Mirror* reported in April 1980; "Tonight's charity show served two purposes. One was to rake cash for Cure, the drug rehabilitation organisation, and the other was to rub the authorities' noses in it as much as possible. The three Stranglers who still retain their liberty understandably feel naffed off by the ludicrous decision to put Hugh Cornwell behind bars. The wisdom of that decision, which has made Cornwell a martyr, was questioned most strongly by drummer Jet Black who said 'They say we have a drug problem in this country — that's wrong. It's a police problem.' The evening will remain a landmark for other reasons as well as being the night The Stranglers played with one member behind bars: it is also a celebration of fifty years life for the grand old Rainbow and it'll be remembered particularly for Hazel O'Connor. For my money, the slight and elegant form topped with the distinctive fuzzy blonde locks offered the most compulsive listening of the evening. Hazel was on stage with her own band as I arrived, but the volume and quality were so distorted that constructive criticism was impossible, However, she took the opportunity to prove her latent talents on vocal chords and body when she came on to do the honours to the last number. 'Grip', with the grim-faced Stranglers. Being Hugh's bird an' that helped, as her familiarity with the material left other participants with a lot to be desired, but, unlike the only *visually* entertaining Toyah, the girl can sing. 'Hanging Around' was given a new slant when a cardboard cut-out, presumably representing Hugh, was towered to keep Hazel company in the middle of the stage which reminded me of a deserted car park — a car park with tons of atmosphere admittedly. Hugh must be doing a lot of hanging around at the moment himself. I must admit I don't actually like The Stranglers, even less the hordes of neanderthal camp-followers, but the array of stars who turned up to help out made the evening."

"To name names they included the talents of Ian Dury, looking uncomfortable with 'Peaches' and 'Bear Cage' but he did get the biggest cheer of the evening: Richard Jobson doing his best impersonation of a lounge lizard with that incredible hair cut on 'Bring On The Nubiles' and succeeding with the song's vocals into the bargain; a wasted, almost skeletal Peter Hammill (late of Van Der Graaf Generator) and Steve Hillage, who leant a little much-needed class to the guitar work. Phil Daniels, Toyah and Wilko floundered around with 'Toiler', 'Duchess' (devoted to the wife of the judge who sent Hugh Cornwell down) and 'Dead Loss Angeles'. The pace was relentless, hardly a pause for breath already, and the sound was better than a poke in the eye with a sharp stick. All praise to the show's organisers for choreographing all those wayward souls into something that definitely resembled order. The cavemen were really doing their nuts for the climax of '5 Minutes', 'Something Better Change' and 'Down In The Sewer'. No one was pretending that this was supposed to be a definitive musical exercise but the week's rehearsals paid off, giving audience and musicians a good laff as well as making a bit of bread for a worthy cause. That and the undoubted ritualistic incineration of our archaic judicial system on a musical pyre. Oh and another thing about Stranglers fans while I'm on the subject — some are so young and female that their dads come to collect them in the car after the gig, judging by the long line of double parked cars and apprehensive faces outside. They must think it's a clever way of protecting their little girls from any nasty rough Meninblack."

In fact, it was apparently the case that Cornwell had the support of many fellow artists whilst he was in prison. *Record Mirror* reported in April 1980; "Kate Bush apparently asked Stranglers manager Ian Grant for Hugh Cornwell's phone number in Pentonville. Somebody had to explain that between the Jacuzzi treatment, the massage sessions, the Cordon Bleu cooking, the manicuring of toenails and sunlamp treatment, Pentonville doesn't give its customers time to talk all day on the phone. The wonderful people of HM prison have also decided to stop giving Hugh Cornwell letters since they claim it's got out of hand. So save your stamps."

It seems that even whilst in prison, Cornwell didn't lose focus when it came to his ambitions for music. *Record Mirror* reported in May 1980; "Hugh Cornwell has recently been hard at work producing the Tea Set, a St Albans-based band he heard while listening to the John Peel show when he was doing time in Pentonville Prison."

When asked if he felt that his time in prison was something that had to happen, Cornwell told *New Musical Express* in September 1982; "Now it's over, yes, in a way I do feel that. It was a very good learning experience. My attitude to certain illegal substances was flippant and actually rather silly. It brought home to me the dependence others had on me. In a group, if you're out of action you're affecting them."

In June 1980, The Stranglers made a memorable appearance in Nice. As one of the UK tabloids put it that month, "Punk rock stars The Stranglers were behind bars last night after a riot at a concert. The four-man British group were accused of deliberately urging their audience to wreck the concert hall. They are likely to spend the weekend in a French jail before a court hearing tomorrow. The group were arrested at their French Riviera hotel after walking out of the show at Nice University because of a power failure. Students threw metal barriers through floor to ceiling windows when the band complained about the university. Police allege that one member of the group said to the audience 'I urge you to break everything'. The controversial foursome are Hugh Cornwell, Jet Black, Dave Greenfield and Jean-Jacques Burnel. The Stranglers' manager, Ian Grant, said in London last night 'We have been trying to get a lawyer to see them but it appears that there is no obligation on the police to let them have representation until forty-eight hours after arrest'."

Details were reported on: "Keyboard player Dave Greenfield was later released but the other three — Hugh Cornwell, Jet Black and Jean-Jacques Burnel, were all charged with inciting a riot and held in prison. The band's manager, Ian Grant, was flying to France at the beginning of this week to arrange bail but at press time it was still not clear whether the band would have to remain in France until the trial came up and whether their upcoming British tour would have to be postponed."

According to the university, the cost of the damage came

to £10,000 which of course, would equate to a lot more today. Trees on the campus grounds were set alight and several plate glass windows were smashed. It posed a huge risk to The Stranglers' freedom in terms of how at the time, the statuary penalty for incitement to cause a riot was for a minimum of one year and a maximum of five years.

In a 1982 interview with the BBC, Jet Black offered an interesting angle on why the riot in Nice may have been a self-fulfilling prophecy for those who were keen to fuel rumours before The Stranglers had even turned up; "We were booked to play a concert in this university and the day before we arrived in Nice, the local newspaper had run a story about The Stranglers' European tour, and that everywhere we were going there were riots and vandalism. I imagine what happened at that point was that the university authorities had read this and thought 'Hell, we've got them playing here tomorrow night' and they decided to find a way of cancelling the gig. Well, of course, they were under contract and it wasn't that simple. And what they decided to do was to refuse us access to electricity, which is absurd. Consequently, we were faced with a situation of trying to run all our equipment without a mains power supply. To overcome this we hired a generator, and when the generator arrived, they refused to allow it in. Eventually we managed to get a limited supply of electricity, but it wasn't enough to run all the equipment. Our sound engineer advised us that if we cut down on everything, we could probably get away with it. So we went ahead and tried to play the gig. And after a few minutes playing, everything overloaded and cut out after about ten minutes. It was obvious that we couldn't continue. So we made an announcement to the people and told them exactly what had happened, that we couldn't play the gig because they refuse to give us the electricity supply. We said 'Don't blame us for this, go and ask the university what they're doing. We don't know.' And having said that, the audience just completely wrecked the place, tore it apart and departed. Then the police arrived after it was all over and said, 'We've got to blame someone for this' so they blamed us for it."

On balance, with the advantage of hindsight and the fact that everything turned out okay in the end, Black said in later years; "In the end, a large fine was split between us and the university, but we laughed all the way to the bank. Before that, we were unknown in France. From then on, we played to packed houses."

At the time though, the incident looked set to affect the upcoming tour dates. *Melody Maker* reported: "The Stranglers' UK tour — due to open at London's Rainbow on July 8th — may be in jeopardy as a result of the riots in Nice… they were due to play in Athens on Thursday, but even if allowed bail they may not be allowed out of France. If bail is refused it could be up to three months before the case comes to court."

New Musical Express reported in July 1980; "The Stranglers' British tour goes ahead next week on schedule — and it's likely that more dates will be added to those already announced. The tour was salvaged last Friday when the three members who'd been in a French jail for almost a week on a charge of inciting violence — Hugh Cornwell, Jet Black and Jean-Jacques Burnel — were released, the first two unconditionally and Burnel on a bail of 100,000 francs (about £10,000). The accused are now required to report back to the court when summoned — probably in October — either to face trial, have the charges dropped or be re-bailed. They are hoping that by that time the court will be prepared to settle for a fine rather than a jail sentence."

"Speaking from his Nice hotel on Friday, manager Ian Grant told NME: 'Even our lawyer was surprised when the boys were freed so quickly. At best, we thought they'd be held until Monday. At worst they could have been in custody until October. The prosecution pulled all the usual strokes. They even raised the age-old issue of Jean-Jacques' national service in France, but fortunately we had the documents with us to prove he was exempt. Apparently they also contacted Interpol to get details of the band's record in other countries, but the telex didn't come through with the information in time for the court hearing — which is just as well!' There is no question of The Stranglers not surrendering to their bail in October, though it seems that, if found guilty, the least they can expect is a fine of the same amount, which allegedly is the extent of the damage caused at Nice University where the trouble occurred."

"The main worry, said Grant, is over Burnel — because it was he who spoke to the audience in French, and is therefore regarded by the police as the main culprit. But the band still insist that they in no way incited the riot, and hope to prove that this was not an isolated instance (British band Screen Idols had a similar experience with under-power generators when they played Nice University at the end of last year, though there were no riots or police involved). The question of The Stranglers' finances is also causing concern. The present hassles come on top of Cornwell's jail sentence in March and the civil action in which the band have been involved, But Grant insisted that The Stranglers will continue come what may — even if their company is forced into liquidation. The band cancelled their Athens concert, because they weren't freed in time to make the necessary ferry bookings. But they were playing in Italy yesterday and tonight (Thursday) — then it's a show in Palma on Friday, back to Italy on Saturday and home for their UK tour starting at the London Rainbow next Tuesday."

Record Mirror reported in July 1980; "The Stranglers have been forced to cancel their concert at the Aberdeen Capitol on July 19th, after the hall's management withdrew the booking. Said promoter John Giddings, 'They seem more prepared to believe what they read in the Sunday papers than anything else. The hall insisted on cancelling the show ten days ago after reading about the incident in Nice and there's nothing we can do... They don't seem to accept the law that someone is innocent until they're proved guilty, so the fans in Aberdeen will have to be disappointed.' But the rest of the concerts on the tour will go ahead as planned, and there have also been some new dales added. It now goes: Blackburn King George's Hall July 21st, Manchester Apollo 22nd, and Stoke-on-Trent Kings Hall 24th. The group returned to Britain earlier this week after a series of European concerts, and three (not just one as previously reported) of The Stranglers will have to appear in the French courts in Nice in September on a charge of "inciting a riot". Said drummer Jet Black, as he arrived, 'The prison experience in Nice was the worst I've ever been through. We were locked up in the police station for a day without food or water'."

It comes across that no matter what was said about them, The Stranglers managed to maintain a pragmatic approach. Regarding the negative press coverage, Cornwell told BBC Radio in January 1983; "At times it's worked for us and at times it's worked against us. All press is like water off a duck's back. Not to insult the whole journalism business, I don't think press really can turn anyone on or off anything they like. If they read bad press about someone they like they're gonna say, 'Oh, it's a pack of lies'. And if they read good press about someone they don't like they're gonna say, 'Oh, *this* is a pack of lies'. It's just something to occupy their time. You need something to read on the loo."

Dave Greenfield told *Strangled* in 1982; "I'm totally, as a rule, one hundred percent anti press. I find that whatever you say they will twist around and in one particular case one of the Sunday papers virtually reversed everything I said. They just wanted sensational stories. That was a few years ago. I generally now avoid giving interviews if I possibly can. There's no point — your point of view is put forward, the reporter changes it to his, the editor changes it again, and goodness knows how many other times it happens down the line. Nowadays I make it a point not to read the music press because I know that whatever I read about whoever just isn't going to be factual. We learned that the hard way. Unless there's an article that someone has particularly recommended I read. When the polls come out I grab a copy as a rule — for the last three or four years I've been number one in the NME keyboards poll. Although the first year I came in it was at something like number four and Hugh was in it too — as a keyboard player! People didn't know too much about us in those days. We checked it with them and they said the votes were definitely there — unless they were covering themselves of course." (Notably in this interview, Greenfield was talking to *Strangled*, a fanzine that The Stranglers were actively involved in the production of).

Jet Black told the BBC in 1982; "I love to pick up a newspaper and read about the bad guys. And whether it's true or not doesn't really interest me. It's a good read."

There was more unfortunate news as *New Musical Express* reported in November 1980: "Latest mishap to befall The Stranglers is the theft of all their gear — and that means all, right down to Dave Greenfield's custom-built keyboards — half-inched from their van (the van went too but was later recovered) after a show at New York's Ritz, in the early stages of the band's US tour. Not only that, but the tour's had to be shortened anyway so that J.J. can face his "incitement to riot" charges in France at the end of the month, result of those disturbances at Nice University last spring. Being fairly optimistic about the outcome, the group plan a Christmas gig in London although their agent says, 'It would be unwise to take anything for granted because they must be the world's unluckiest band.' So unlucky we're not even going to throw in a gratuitous insult." Ouch!

Regarding the problems of 1980 Greenfield told *Sounds* in January 1981; "There's always been problems before but this year certainly had the worst. The years before kind of pale into insignificance beside it, but I think it's changing now slowly. The crew have got that feeling as well, I don't know why. Things are starting to pick up again, I feel. Our luck will get better."

It is clear that when Cornwell spoke in the same interview, the only way was up. When asked about what kind of success The Stranglers were looking for, he replied; "The success that means buying some new fucking equipment. We'll deal with the rest as it comes."

Prior to the release of *La Folie*, there was everything to play for. Just days before the album began to make waves, a journalist wrote for *Record Mirror* in November 1981; "The Stranglers' waning record sales: As businessmen, it must be said, The Stranglers are not the world's best. It has never really been considered good tactics to get on the wrong side of people like the BBC for instance. Or to put it another way "don't bite the hand that feeds". It's now over two years since The Stranglers had their last major hit ('Duchess'), but also *Meninblack* didn't chart as well as previous albums."

By late 1981, The Stranglers clearly had the desire to move on from what had been quite a bleak period. Jet Black told the *Liverpool Echo* in October 1981; "Look, we are happy. We are having fun. We are not strange. People change. We all do. Why do people think we are some kind of depressive masochists?... You are conditioned in your life by your surroundings. There's no doubt about that. At the moment everything is going right for us. The pendulum has swung... Everything, and I mean *everything* seemed to be getting in our way. We had all the hassle in France, problems with records, all sorts of bad press. You name it, we had it... I'll say we were paranoid. Being in rock is a very schizophrenic existence in a way, and you tend to imagine lots of things, perhaps, but we certainly kept coming across cold hard facts — facts that seemed to indicate that

27

someone, somewhere had it in for us."

In January 1982, Cornwell told *The Daily Mirror* about how The Stranglers' *Meninblack* era hadn't particularly been a positive experience: "All that weird stuff nearly killed off the band. In two years we had the most unbelievable run of bad luck — friends died, managers kept leaving us and tours had to be cancelled."

Record Mirror considered in November 1981; "Let's face it, life as a Strangler can't have been a lot of fun lately. Apart from having become the band that everybody loves to hate, the past eighteen months has been particularly rife with catastrophes for them. The mere fact that they are still together as a band at the end of this disastrous period is a survival success story in itself. The "strange chain of events", as they have become to be known, can be traced back to the point where The Stranglers began to take a more than passing interest in the Meninblack on their *Raven* LP. Since then, the regularity with which their misfortunes seem to have occurred is almost too uncanny to be true."

"Firstly, there were the well publicised events such as Hugh Cornwell's two-month residency in Pentonville nick, the whole band's detention in Nice and of course the theft of all their equipment in the USA. In between all these, however, there were numerous bizarre happenings, some of which involved the serious illness — even death — of some of The Stranglers' closest associates. It is not surprising, therefore, that The Stranglers are keen to drop the whole Meninblack saga. What is perhaps surprising is that they have re-emerged with an album that is basically a compilation of love songs. Admittedly, they aren't conventional love songs (there are ones about a nun's love of God, a dictator's love of power and even one about the fans' love of John Lennon "post mortem" as it were). But it seems ironic, taking into account much of the band's history and the criticism directed at them, that they should give so much of their attention to the subject of love."

By the time *La Folie* was released in November 1981, it is understandable as to why The Stranglers may have felt that fate had the knives out for them, and why the album served the band well in terms of empowering them to turn the tables.

Chapter Two

The Making of La Folie

*L*a *Folie* was recorded over three weeks at The Manor —
an estate near Oxford, owned by Virgin boss Richard
Branson, and famous for having hosted Mike Oldfield
when he made *Tubular Bells* (1973). The Stranglers spent 16th
August to 6th September at The Manor. Another week was
spent at London's Good Earth studios on the mixing.

As was the case on The Stranglers' previous two albums,
The Raven and *The Meninblack*, the band worked with Steve
Churchyard. *La Folie*'s final sound mix was done by Tony
Visconti. Cornwell described him as having "gold" ears.

When asked why The Stranglers chose to work with
Visconti, Burnel told *Black & White* in 1982; "Even if we do our
own production, it's always worth having an outside opinion.
He had no part in the production and hadn't gone through those
three weeks of recording at The Manor. That way, he had a
totally objective approach, outside the politics of the group.
He brought a fresh ear, separate from our universe. And what's
more, we knew what he was capable of. Everything went well,
he did nothing dramatic. It's rare that a guy as famous as him
accepts to do that kind of work. It's new in the business to have
a famous producer do the mixing. It's never been done before.
Not a bad system."

Prior to setting to work at The Manor, The Stranglers
worked on the songs at Jet Black's house. In just a living room
of fifteen square metres, the keyboards were at one end, the
drums at the other, and then bass and guitars were in the middle.

Notably, some of the material that made it onto *La Folie* hadn't been written all that long before the band started recording. When asked if they had any new songs, Burnel told *Strangled* during the first half of 1981; "We have rehearsed about half a dozen but we are trying to get together about twenty before we begin recording in July. I don't know if we'll have the time but at the moment we are headed in the right direction. We are thinking of recording in France. Personally, I hope to get my revenge by recording in Nice."

The lead vocals on *La Folie* are covered by Cornwell and Burnel. Greenfield told *Strangled* in 1982; "I do sing though I'm not singing anything on *La Folie* — only harmonies — but I've averaged about one song per album so far, and harmony work of course. I wouldn't like to sing all the time though — it limits my movement with the mic there obviously. I'd have to leave out all the synthesisers and things I've got on the right of me. I would never be able to reach them and sing."

Although each of the songs on *La Folie* are connected by the concept of love, many subjects are explored within that theme, thus keeping the album lyrically very broad. It makes sense that the album turned out that way in view of how when making it, The Stranglers spoke of the theme from a wide and philosophical stance.

Jet Black wrote an extensive essay for *Strangled* in 1981. That which follows is merely a fraction of his contribution. He went on to give many examples in order to get his main point across but in essence, this was his angle: "With a new Stranglers' alum entitled *La Folie* (The Madness) on the verge of release, it occurs to me that *Strangled* readers may like a hint or two at the kind of notions which motivated the concept. The concept or theme of the album is love. A study of love. A repudiation of love or, to put it another way, perhaps there is no such thing as love: It is one of the many illusions of mankind which he steadfastly refuses to recognise. An analogy I find most appropriate is that love is *The King's New Clothes*. You must have heard that children's fairytale about the two con men who sold the king a new "invisible" suit. To the horror of his court, the king strutted around stark naked urging his subjects to admire his new suit, utterly convinced that he was wearing one. Hans Andersen was no fool. Like Lewis Carroll (and many others), Hans Andersen used the "children's story" as his cover for some home truths that would have been quite unacceptable to the unenlightened thinkers of the day. I don't think that there can be much doubt that the majority of people on this planet give blind credence to the notion of love with the same unquestioning stupidity as Hans Andersen's king. After all, I hear them say, 'How can the entire world be wrong and you be right?'. Easy; it would not be the first time that one man had changed the status quo."

"There was a time when everyone believed that the sun revolved around the earth until suddenly the telescope was invented. The scholars and theologians around the globe had to eat their words. As usual, they did this as slowly and cowardly as possible. And so it is with love. Alas, the age of enlightenment is not imminent, but if such an era ever dawns, we will be able to gloat at the ensuing theological locative banquet. It seems to me that love is one of those ideas that was given out thousands of years ago when someone was going around giving out "ideas", but no one can remember what love was supposed to be. The trouble with love is that it is such a nice concept. Perhaps this is the reason for its universal acceptability. But is it any more real than the king's new clothes? What do we mean by the word "love"? At first it may seem a simple matter, but the dictionary reveals a plethora of meaning to this simple sounding four-letter word. After only the most cursory or researches, it appears that the word "love" is used and misused in a myriad of different contexts. So when he says 'Darling I love you', is there anything intrinsically different from when he says 'I love to drink beer'?"

"I have canvassed opinion on this and it seems that what people mean when they use the word is really what matters. I find that people always react the same way in their understanding of these two phrases, i.e. 'I love to drink beer' is not really about love, but simply a revelation about that which makes him happy or, if you like, in this example he loves himself. The consensus seems to be that this example isn't about love at all, but is simply an acceptable misuse of the word. On the other hand, 'Darling I love you' is clearly regarded as an expression of love, i.e. the pouring out of this invisible "stuff" from one person to the loved one. I find it interesting that Hans Andersen's king was also fooled by the invisible."

"After many years of experience and though rounded off by recent research, I am now firmly of the opinion that that which is popularly regarded as love does actually exist but it isn't love by popular understanding of the word. In fact, love is the exact opposite of what it is supposed to be. Love is selfishness, egocentricism, greed, lust. But that isn't love is it? No. Exactly; there is no such thing as love except for love for oneself. And since love of oneself isn't in fact love, i.e. the outpouring of that invisible "stuff", I have to conclude that there isn't any such thing as love."

Black told the *Liverpool Echo* in October 1981; "Our new album is a total concept about love. It's called *La Folie* and is all about the many aspects of love. After all the things I've seen and experienced in the world, I have to ask myself is there really such a thing as "love" and if so, what is "love"? The way things happen, there never seems to be love for love's sake — it seems to be more about power, passion, and pain. That's why we've called the album *La Folie* — love's folly, you see? I'm absolutely delighted with it. We've got Tony Visconti in to do the mixing and I think for the first time ever on a Stranglers album he has got the clear distinct sound we wanted. In the past we have been too close to the music ourselves."

When asked how it came to be that The Stranglers got hooked onto the subject of love, Cornwell told *Record Mirror* in November 1981; "Just thinking about things, you know. Everyone was saying 'you don't write love songs do you?' And we said 'No, we'll never write a love song.' The closest we ever got to it was 'Bring On The Nubiles' and also 'School Mam', that's a love song. I started thinking about that and I thought, 'Wouldn't it be good to write a collection of songs about love — but have them describing the complete folly of it, and the complete madness of it — and the things people do in the name of it.' Like in France, for example, they have crime passionnel, which is if someone kills someone in the name of love, they can be let off the guillotine, or whatever the punishment is. It's not called murder, it's called crime passionnel. It's fantastic when you think of it. In fact there's a case just happening in France now."

Burnel told *Black & White* in 1982; "Madness is one of those things which puts us out of order. This distraction which makes us commit irrational, destructive and nihilistic acts. Irrational like so-called love which in all its forms is only a pretence. Madness is not an illness but rather an attack, a surprise attack like Pearl Harbour. It shocks, unconsciously. It is said to blind even the most sane. Only the French word could express all this. We did look for a English word but even "madness" isn't the same as the word "folie". Many people in England haven't really understood... Nothing is a problem for The Stranglers. Madness is only a phenomenon which fascinates us. All around us people make mistakes, do stupid things that the automata we are supposed to be shouldn't ever do. Things like pride, love or even war. The next war will be the greatest "folie". We give different names to all those pretences but they are expressions of madness. Apart from that, madness isn't a symbol as such, like a raven or a rat. No, it's a phenomenon we have studied and observed under the microscope."

The opening track, 'Non Stop' was actually supposed to be called — as the lyrics go — 'Non Stop Nun' but the last word was dropped from the title at the last minute. Black's drums introduce the track and then a distinctive melody comes in straight away. The message of the song relates to the idea that if God is a delusion, then it is a powerful, man-made mistake. For the writing of the song, Burnel put a number of ideas forward for bass parts and there was one in particular that Cornwell liked straight away.

At the beginning of the second track, 'Everybody Loves You When You're Dead', there is a musical conversation between the bass and the guitar before the drums and synths come in at the same time — they play the same phrase throughout the duration of the song. As with the opening track, the vocals come across as somewhat sardonic as the lyrics explore the phenomenon of how when a person dies, people suddenly seem to take more of an interest in them. In relation to this, on the inner cover of *La Folie*'s artwork, there are pictures of Che Guevara and John Lennon. In later years Cornwell spoke of how he has always been fascinated by human behaviour and that the topic for the song worked well in the context of the album's theme.

Cornwell championed the third track, 'Tramp' as a single but the other members weren't so keen on the idea. All the same, the interplay on all of the instruments in an almost jazz-like manner grows into a solid rock song with a refrain of harmonic vocals. Even the bass guitar part has a strongly melodic structure. The theme of the song is in how someone like a tramp can enjoy a love for the freedom of having no responsibilities.

The fourth track, 'Let Me Introduce You To The Family', was the first choice of promo single for *La Folie*. The rhythm section is almost in the style of disco but the heaviness of the song is that which could be pogoed to. The bass is heavy and pumping throughout. On the album artwork, the picture next to the lyrics shows a family gathering like the ones from Francis Ford Coppola's *Godfather* films. The idea is in line with the song's lyrics that refer to the Mafia's love for the family and how such behaviour can create a gang-like mentality. On the cover of the single release of the song, there are pictures of automatic rifles from around the time of the American Prohibition.

It was through the live performances of the song that the fierce mood of it really came across. All in all though, considering the theme and style of the song, it's hardly surprising that it didn't fare well in the charts; it got to number forty-two in the UK and then dropped out soon after.

Cornwell's inspiration for the lyrics for the song came from when he was working in education. A student of his insisted that he should meet their family. He was introduced to a happy and cohesive group of people. It was in contrast to his expectations based on what he had experienced with his own family. In later years, Cornwell told of how he appreciates his family but at the time of meeting this student's family, there was a sense of envy.

The single was reviewed in the *Liverpool Echo* in October 1981; "Godfathers of punk return with an offer you can't refuse — full of fun and a hit." Notably by 1981 The Stranglers were still being merged in under punk. In all fairness though, musically, 'Let Me Introduce You To The Family' certainly does have a rather punk-ish quality to it. In the same month, the *Newcastle Evening Chronicle* reviewed the single; "Tight and mean, but not The Stranglers at their menacing, disturbing best."

When asked, "Why write a song on the Mafia?" Burnel told *Black & White* in 1982; "Hugh wanted to identify himself ironically with a child of the Family, because the Mafia, same as The Stranglers, is an organisation based on itself. An organisation which takes on the rest of the world. All cliques interest us. Things like gangs, the Finchley Boys, the Templars, the Freemasons. The Stranglers are all of these."

'Ain't Nothin' To It' is almost in the style of a rap. The song's lyrics are derived from what was originally speech. The song is about the love that people can have for a life of debauchery (whether celebrated or just taken for granted as part of a day-to-day existence). The music is funky and dissonant-sounding and when all of the instruments fall briefly silent, Burnel's bass comes in in a frenzied solo.

Explaining the use of Milton Mezzrow's words for 'Ain't Nothin' To It', Cornwell wrote passionately for *Strangled* in 1982; "Milton Mezzrow is hailed as the greatest white jazz clarinettist that ever lived. During his lifetime he played with most of the great black musicians of the twentieth century. He learned to play the clarinet whilst serving numerous jail sentences for petty crimes (some of which he did not commit) when he was a young man. It seemed to him to be the most constructive use of his time inside. Throughout his colourful life he was constantly let down by white people and helped by black people. One of his first musical engagements was leading a band in one of Al Capone's bars outside Chicago. He became a close friend of "Satchmo" Louis Armstrong and worked on many musical arrangements with him. After several heavy liaisons with drugs, formed and led the first "two-tone" band in the world, playing in New York on Broadway to rave reviews. The band's career was short-lived, falling foul of the US Nazi party. Mezzrow was probably most famous for his contributions to Negro jive talk in Harlem, which enabled the black people in the area to talk openly about drugs — mostly marijuana — without fear of being understood by passers-by. Mezzrow dealt weed from street corners for several years in Harlem and to his death always maintained that he was more black than white. (For reference, see *Really The Blues* by Milton Mezzrow and Bernard Wolfe)." Notably, Cornwell didn't mention that in actual fact, the lyrics to 'Ain't Nothing To It' were taken from a conversation that Mezzrow had with around eight other people!

'The Man They Love To Hate' is about the love for the hatred that people can have on men. The interplay between guitar and synth is strong on this track, as are the intrinsic drumming rhythms. The bass has echo on it in certain parts of the song and this is something that was carried across for the live performances of it. When playing the intro to 'The Man They Love To Hate' on stage, Burnel used a foot switch (a Yamaha Analogue Delay Model E1010) to create an echoing delay.

When Jet Black was in Los Angeles in 1982, he noticed how K Roq radio station kept playing 'The Man They Love To Hate'. Apparently it was done in homage to the Program Controller when the employee pay cheques bounced!

The opening track of side two — 'Pin Up' — would arguably have made an excellent single with its catchy memorable melody and upbeat synth pop feel to it. Vitally, it is danceable and would have been right at home in the charts of the early eighties that were heralding similar sounds from the new wave. When Tony Visconti set to work on the material, Dave Greenfield's piano contribution was passed through a synthesiser. Next to the lyrics on the album art is a picture of Marilyn Monroe.

'It Only Takes Two To Tango' contains a range of interesting vocals; normal range stuff from Cornwell and Burnel as well as moments of harmony that don't sound too different to barbershop singing. In line with the rhythmic quirks of the song, Black's drumming is impressive. The theme of love on this song exists in the form of how war can be disguised as something of a dance. On the album art, next to the lyrics is an image of the presidents of the USA and the USSR in a ballroom dancing pose together (Reagan wears the man's suit whilst Brezhnev wears the ball gown). The complexity of the song — both vocally and from a rhythmic perspective — is such that it was rarely performed live due to the sheer technical demand of it.

At face value, the lyrics to 'Golden Brown' are ambiguous. Convenient really, considering that what it's really about was initially concealed; The Stranglers didn't want it to be censored from radio airplay upon its release.

Regarding the song, Cornwell told BBC Radio in February 1982; "What it really represents is the ultimate scam; it's a complete collection of blank verse which is presented to the listener to interpret whichever way they want, and whatever people come up with as the idea behind the song shows exactly what they're preoccupied with. A mental test that a guy called Rorschach developed called the Rorschach test — which involved a blank piece of paper, some ink blots on it, some smudging, folding the paper over and then presenting it to a mental patient — they just come out with all their hang-ups."

When asked what he envisioned in his own interpretation of the lyrics, Cornwell did the ultimate in diversion by talking of "beaches and sand and sunsets. People react differently to different colours. If you show them a red, there are emotional responses different to green. Green is calming and red is quite exciting. Sensual, so I mean, brown is a deeper kind of red. I was trying to write about all the things, those sort of emotions, that brown can give you. When I see brown, that's all the things that I think of."

When asked about 'Golden Brown' in September 1982, he explained; "Contrary to what is sometimes said, it's not about heroin. There's a lot of different things it could be about. People used to do this with old Beatles songs, finding cryptic messages. One Dutch journalist even thought 'Golden Brown' was about the white slave trade — you know, 'How long have The Stranglers been into white slavery?' Unbelievable."

Of course, it is now common knowledge that 'Golden

Brown' is indeed about — among other things — heroin but at the time, it is understandable as to why it may have been in the band's best interests to promote a different story. And in all fairness, The Stranglers were often asked about the meanings behind their songs and were probably very used to dispelling all kinds of weird and wonderful theories. Cornwell said that one fan wrote to them and insisted that "There was a secret message on 'Enough Time' on *Black And White*, a Morse code message that said, 'SOS This is Planet Earth. We are fucked'."

Before the lyrics of 'Golden Brown' were announced as being about heroin, the single was listed as Record Of The Week on BBC Radio Two, an impressive achievement considering that usually, the station wouldn't touch anything from a band even slightly associated with punk.

In January 1982, *The Daily Mirror* said of 'Golden Brown'; "The Stranglers' current single — the biggest hit for a long time — is a mellow love song, in contrast to the menacing music of the band's past."

Cornwell said; "The single has surprised quite a few people. It's not all that common for a Stranglers song to be chosen as David Hamilton's Record Of The Week on Radio Two! But we've always experimented with varied types of music, and this is just one more direction. The violence in our music was misunderstood — it was always meant to be tongue-in-cheek."

It's nice to think that the success of 'Golden Brown' perhaps served as something of a platform for The Stranglers to better explain that their earlier music wasn't made with the intention to offend or cause confrontation (not that back in 1977, the media attention to it had done the band any harm on the publicity front).

Cornwell insists to this day that the drugs reference is just one level to the song's meaning. At the time of writing it he also had his then-girlfriend from South America in mind.

Decades after the song's release, the scope to be more

candid about its meaning afforded Cornwell to explain in 2017; "I think looking back it was an ode to heroin. Maybe ode isn't the right word. It was a lovely period of time and romantic and you get into the romanticism thing. A lot of people get into the romanticism of drug-taking because of the old English poets, Shelley and Coleridge. They were drug addicts. And really the best poetry you ever come up with is when you're stone cold sober. I think when people hear the lyrics, not knowing whether it's about heroin, they hear the romance in them. But really it's saying be careful. Heroin was a dangerous thing so I tried to put that in the lyrics... We would have got to number one, but big-mouth-Burnel decided to tell the press what it was about, and suddenly it was removed from all the playlists and I said 'thank you very much!' I would have waited until it got to number one, and then said." ('Golden Brown' was kept off the top spot first by Tight Fit's 'The Lion Sleeps Tonight' and then The Jam's 'A Town Called Malice'/'Precious').

That's not to say that getting to number two in the UK is a prohibitive position though. One paper reported of 'Golden Brown'; "The single from the album has so far sold close on a million copies in the UK and is the bestselling British single so far in 1982. *Melody Maker* gave it a number one listing and it lasted a total of fourteen weeks on the British charts. 'Golden Brown', has, so far, achieved top ten listings in Holland, Belgium, France, Italy, Germany and Australia."

On balance, Burnel didn't let the cat out of the bag straight away. When asked if he was able to say what 'Golden Brown' was about, he told *Black & White* in 1982; "I can't reveal anything on that subject, for the time being. We think it's certainly going to be a great success in England. Without doubt The Stranglers' greatest hit to date. And if I had to reveal what 'Golden Brown' is about I'd be taking a risk. The four of us have decided not to reveal anything to anyone, otherwise, ask me again at the end of January."

When the record company wanted to reject the song, The Stranglers insisted on a contractual clause to oblige them to put it out. Speaking to MTV in 1990, Burnel said; "The nature of the business is such that if you are not in some kind of league table then you're finished. People are always very keen to write you off. I think one of the greatest pleasures I had was when we had a song which no one wanted to release, 'Golden Brown'. We wanted it released and they said, 'Well, a) it's not a dance record, b) It doesn't sound like The Stranglers.' We insisted on it being released and despite the record company, it was a massive success in terms of single success only... it was a real two fingers up to the record company."

There is debate amongst music scholars as to which time signature best represents some parts of the song: some say that the main harpsichord theme (the part sans vocals) is in 13/4 (or even 13/8) whilst others would describe it as three bars of 3/4 followed by a single bar of 4/4. Both ways of looking at it ultimately add up to the same number of beats but three lots of 3/4 plus a single bar of 4/4 at the end of a phrase is arguably a more relatable way in which to count along to the rhythm (123,123,123,1234). The parts of the song that include vocals remain in 3/4 (Cornwell figured that it made more sense to do it this way in order to a) ensure that the piece didn't become too complicated and b) so that complexity for its own sake wouldn't take away from the attractiveness of the piece overall.

Even though 'Golden Brown' itself was written within half an hour, Dave Greenfield's part had been cooking in his head for some time prior. Upon the keyboard player's passing in 2020, Cornwell posted on Twitter that he'd made "the difference between The Stranglers and every other punk band".

Strangled reported in 1982 that Greenfield had mentioned to them that "an original part of 'Second Coming' in 13/4 time which was never used: this was saved and forms the basis of the tune for 'Golden Brown' with the addition of new material plus lyrics."

Greenfield told *Strangled* in 1982; "Music just appears in my head. I never write it down. I remember it or tape it. If I had to write it down I could do it but it would take a fair time to write it down and then if I found I'd forgotten it, it would take a fair bit of time to decipher the notation... I listen to any sort of music provided it's written well or played well. No particular favourite bands — I try to avoid that because I might subconsciously start playing like them. So I won't listen to one particular style or one particular keyboard player. Really I listen to very little music as a rule."

A journalist reported in *International Musician & Recording World* in November 1982; "It was interesting to discover that the harpsichord on 'Golden Brown' was the real thing and not an electronic replica. It wasn't even an electric model with inbuilt pickups and was mic'd up in the true tradition of yesteryear. Hugh reckoned that certain numbers lend themselves to definite instruments and for this song, the harpsichord was the obvious choice."

Directed by Lindsey Clennell, the music video for 'Golden Brown' depicts members of the band as performers for a fictional Radio Cairo and as explorers in an Arabian country. As well as pyramids, the video includes cuts to stock footage of the Mir-i-Arab Madrasa in Bukhara, the Shah Mosque in Isfahan, the Great Sphinx, feluccas sailing, Bedouins riding, and camel racing in the United Arab Emirates. The performance scenes were filmed in the Leighton House Museum in Holland Park, London. The same location would go on to be used in the filming of Spandau Ballet's 'Gold' music video.

In 1983, Cornwell said of working with Lindsey Clennell; "We worked very closely with him. We always maintain a strong control over a video's content because we think it's very important; we want it to show what we want. The worst thing is to leave it in someone's hands totally; you go down to see the final cut and it's nothing like what you imagined. That has happened a couple of times to us. And since that happened, we decided to try and have more control. First you've got a director, then you've got an editor. And if they're both creative people, they're both pulling in different directions. And we try and act as almost like producers in it. We try and make sure that everyone's working on the same film, rather than on their own different films."

On the album's inner cover art, the lyrics to 'How To Find True Love And Happiness In The Present Day' are adorned with hearts to the extent that it looks ironic. It certainly matches the way in which the vocals come across in the song. The lyrics focus on the love of money, power and status in society as a symbol of success in life. They make reference to a man who, upon chasing and accumulating money during his life, comes to realise that he doesn't have enough time to spend it. The song was the last to be composed for *La Folie* and the process with which it was done was standard for The Stranglers. Burnel contributed the basic melody, Cornwell did the lyrics and the composition was ready within a day.

After the phenomenal success of 'Golden Brown', the record company asked The Stranglers for something that they could repeat the success with. Burnel said in later years; "They released ('Golden Brown') at Christmas, expecting it to be drowned in a tsunami of Christmas singles. After it was a hit all over the world, they asked for 'another 'Golden Brown''. So we gave them a seven-minute song in French." The song was 'La Folie'. With lyrics inspired by the Japanese necrophiliac murderer and cannibal Issei Sagawa, it isn't too surprising that it charted at number forty-seven.

'Tramp' had originally been considered as the follow-up single to 'Golden Brown' but 'La Folie' was chosen when Burnel succeeded to convince the rest of the band on it.

When asked if he felt that the single release of 'La Folie'

was a mistake, Cornwell told BBC Radio in January 1983; "I've had a lot of people say that if it would have been in English then it would probably be a lot more acceptable. No, I love the sound of it."

In later years Burnel said; "To the English it was just meaningless Froggy terms. As a single, 'La Folie' bombed, of course. Hugh and the label thought it was madness and wanted 'Tramp' released but I always thought it was healthy to do whatever was least obvious." "I couldn't believe Jean swayed everybody to agree," said Cornwell. "A silly, vain choice. It's in French, for fuck's sake."

Despite its unusual subject matter and its not-exactly-stellar chart positioning, 'La Folie' is demonstrative of where The Stranglers were at musically during that period. The track is abundantly in the style of an eighties synth ballad and with the French-spoken lyrics it sounds like something that wouldn't be out of place from a band more associated with the new romantics. At just over six minutes long, 'La Folie' is a slow and melodically simple song — another reason that made it a risky choice of single. To get radio play of such a number was always going to be a challenge because essentially, it wasn't suitable.

Black & White asked Burnel in 1982; "Jet's work on this album is totally original and subtle. Don't you think that on *La Folie* he has made a step forward and given a new personal dimension to his instrument?" His response: "Oh yeah! In any case he's always kept a low profile. There are drummers who try hard to beat as many skins as possible in the least possible time. That's not really his way of seeing things or of playing. On a track such as 'La Folie', for example, there's hardly any drum but that's exactly what was needed! He is efficient and together. It's rare in a drummer. It's a wisdom of playing which is uncommon nowadays. People now want to put everything they've got into their drums without any interpretation. It's a mistake… On certain tracks like 'How To Find True Love And Happiness In The Present Day' we tell him we would like that kind of style but normally, he interprets things himself on his own. Like on the track 'La Folie'. We waited for the drums but nothing came. We were beginning to worry and then, all of a sudden: tap, tap. Afterwards he told us, 'No, I really can't do anything more on that one.' He really interprets the song as he hears it."

It's a strong possibility that any musical similarities that 'La Folie' may have in common with synth pop and the new romantics were not deliberate imitations. Far from it. Burnel told *Black & White* in 1982; "Orchestral Manoeuvres are quite interesting — for supermarkets. Blood Donor are incredible, a totally unknown band. They've brought out two singles, plus an album which Arista actually refused two years ago. They consisted of two keyboards plus two drummers, an electric drum kit and a normal one. One of the two drummers sang and had a moustache cut in half. They were totally ahead of their time. Unbelievable. Skids I also liked at the beginning. Steel Pulse I still like. Otherwise there are hardly any of our contemporaries that I respect. The Clash, up to a point. Especially Joe Strummer, I like him a lot, he's a good guy. I don't like all their lyrics, but him I instinctively like. The others not really."

Whilst musically, 'La Folie' sounds mellow and tender, the lyrics allude to something horrific. On 11th June, thirty-two-year-old Sagawa (who had moved from Japan to France in order to undertake a PhD in literature) invited a classmate, Renée Hartevelt to have dinner with him at his apartment. It was on the understanding that they would translate poetry together for an assignment. Enchanted by Hartevelt's health and beauty, Sagawa planned to kill and eat her. Considering himself small, weak and ugly, he claimed that he wanted to absorb her energy. After Hartevelt arrived, she began reading poetry at a desk with her back to Sagawa. He shot her in the neck with a rifle. He fainted after the shock of shooting her, but awoke determined to carry out his plan. He had sex with the corpse and when he found himself unable to bite into her skin, he left the apartment to buy a butcher's knife. Upon his return, Sagawa consumed parts of Hartevelt's body; most of her breasts and face either raw or cooked. He opted to store other parts in his refrigerator. He photographed Hartevelt's body after every stage of consumption. Carrying remains of the corpse in two suitcases, Sagawa intended to dump them in a lake in the Bois de Boulogne. He was caught though and was arrested by the police.

Regarding the Sagawa case, Cornwell told *Record Mirror* in November 1981; "There's this Japanese student in Paris who had this passion to eat a young girl: Anyway, last spring he finally got this girl to agree to go out with him. So he took her out, took her back to his flat and he killed her, chopped her up and ate her — and he put the rest of her in the fridge. You might laugh, but this actually happened, there was a big article about it in the *Sunday Times*. The French authorities are freaking out because they don't know what to do with him, because really it's a crime passionnel, so really he should be let off. He had a passion for this person, he loved her so much he wanted to eat her — and he did it. This sort of thing we're fascinated by on *La Folie*, these sort of people, these sort of situations."

When asked if the story of Sagawa was the starting point for *La Folie*, Burnel told *Black & White* in 1982; "No, that anecdote wasn't the basic inspiration for the track or the album. We had already thought about conceiving an LP about love, but we found that this story portrayed exactly what we wanted to express. We already had the music for the track, we had the title and the concept for the album and the song, but we hadn't decided on the words. I was in a studio, reading *The Times* and suddenly I exclaimed 'Unbelievable! Hugh, come and have a look. Perfect, isn't it? This guy has done it for us!'."

The French lyrics, of course, were written by Burnel. Cornwell once described the music as feeling like falling through a large pillow full of feathers. It's a tremendous contrast to the song's subject! It sees the album end on a jarring, thought-provoking note as Burnel continues to repeat in almost a whisper, "La Folie".

When asked if the first part of 'La Folie' — where Sagawa meets his girlfriend — is symbolic of him meeting with madness, Burnel told *Black & White* in 1982; "No, no connection really. It's just about sexual satisfaction, nothing to do with emotion. You meet a girl in the street, you try to pick her up, five minutes later you've made up your mind, without any emotion. The next day, you tiptoe out, boots in hand, without even saying goodbye. No more, no less, without any shades of romance. Totally cold, as many people would wish it. A kind of therapy."

To make the music video for 'La Folie', Cornwell and Burnel went to Paris for a night. They took lots of heroin whilst there which saw them taking a long walk around the Seine. In a trance-like state, they stopped at bars occasionally. The crew simply filmed them walking and talking.

In 1982, Burnel was spending a lot of his free time in France. His parents lived there and he was going out with a French woman. He said at the time, "When I grew up I insisted on being called John 'cos I was ashamed of being French and of my mum speaking in a broad French accent and being kissed in front of the school gates. Inevitably kids want to have a go at you."

With *La Folie* though, he evidently drew upon his French heritage. He said of his vocals on the album's title track; "I worked on that a bit to get the accent perfect. There's some kind of intellectual snobbery in New York arts circles about people wanting to do things in French and it can sound hammy."

Around that time, Burnel had a lot of confidence in the

French music scene overall. He produced one of the top groups in France, Taxi Girl. He explained, "The French are still insecure about modern music. There's a situation where a lot of people want to make music, probably for different reasons than people in England. It's relatively easy here to have a hit, to be a bandwagon jumper. You can be totally obscure and still be this week's alternative chart buster. A lot of people in this country want to make money first of all."

The picture of the anatomical heart on the inside cover of *La Folie* is labelled not with individual parts of the organ but with the names of the people who helped to make the album. This was Cornwell's idea and one inspired by his days in biomedical science.

Regarding the anatomical heart, Burnel told *Black & White* in 1982; "Love is always associated with stupid symbolism such as cupids or that typical, perfectly shaped heart. It's all part of the affront to — and conspiracy against — reality. If everyone sees things as they are, it does not help the system. So people hide the truth behind mystical and romantic expressions, behind symbols which make no sense. We wanted to express just this, through the anatomical heart, which is a reflection of the truth: an incredibly well organised but extremely ugly pump, which has nothing to do with this deceptive mysticism... The only possible love is the love of oneself. All other forms of so-called love are, in fact, the manifestation of that love for oneself. Maternal love, for instance. The mother who feeds, spoils and looks after her child does it because it pleases her and herself only. There is proof that there are those who don't fall into that pattern. Because it disturbs them. Then, instead, they go out on the pick-up and get stoned. Mother Theresa does love saving children but in fact you must realise that for her it's a real inner enjoyment. Otherwise she would give it up. It's like Jet, who one day met a guy who said he'd found happiness. Jet grabbed him. 'Ah! Yeah! How? Tell me, tell me.' 'By pleasing others.'

And Jet realised, after a while, that this bloke was pleasing himself at the same time as pleasing others. Love is totally, definitely selfish, but one dissimulates, one hides and distorts everything."

A spokesperson for Liberty estimated that some 10,000 to 15,000 copies of the 'Golden Brown' single had been pressed with the wrong B-side and distributed prior to the mistake being noticed by the record company. The wrongly used song, 'Everybody Samba', was by Mick Dee, a singer from Sweden and member of the band Music For Boys.

Also, there were some faulty copies of *La Folie* in distribution. Again, a technical error noticed by the record label only after the fact. Liberty's awareness of the problem was such that they were willing to exchange the record for a new copy. One fan complained that he had come across a number of copies of the record — purchased from brand new — where the opening track 'Pin Up' kept jumping.

Reviews

A journalist writing for *Record Mirror* considered in November 1981; "My meetings with Hugh Cornwell have always been pleasant, amiable experiences, this occasion no less so. We begin by listening to the new LP, *La Folie*, during which I notice how mellow The Stranglers are sounding these days. There's nothing here, for example, with the force of songs even as recent as 'Who Wants The World?' or 'Nuclear Device'. At last it looks as though they have mastered the array of styles which has been developing in their music over the last couple of years — the result being that this album is infinitely more accessible than anything they have done since *Black And White*. At one point I jovially remark to Hugh that some of the music on *La Folie* could easily have been written with the Radio Two market in mind, to which he replies that they were really aiming for Radio Three. A slight overstatement perhaps, but it gives you some idea of how polarised The Stranglers are becoming."

Under the heading of "Pop Go The Heavy Guys," *La Folie* was reviewed in the *Atherstone News and Herald*; "It's very hard to remain objective and critical when it comes to reviewing your favourite band. However, The Stranglers' seventh album, *La Folie*, is one that I can honestly and firmly recommend as the best album you will hear this year. Unlike previous releases that have been full of aggression and musical spite, this is unashamedly a pop album. As Teardrop Explodes has consistently proved, "pop" is not a dirty word and The Stranglers further proved this fact on this eleven-track gem which I hope will fill an awful lot of stockings this Christmas."

"Every track — bar one, 'Catastrophe' (sic) — has nice, swirling keyboards and bouncy rhythms as their base, and when complemented with the much-improved vocals of Hugh Cornwell and J.J. Burnel, the sound is likely to appeal to many who in the past have either hated, or been apathetic towards The Stranglers. Songs such as 'Tramp', 'True Love' (sic) and 'Non Stop' would make a refreshing change, if they became singles, to a consistently depressing hit parade. Yet not everything on this album is as light and commercial. The lengthy, excellent title track and the amazing 'Golden Brown' are songs of real quality which will appeal to a more specialised listener and 'The Man They Love To Hate' is The Stranglers at their purest, perfectly blending the old vicious-sounding Stranglers with the more tuneful side of this incredible foursome. *La Folie* is an album anybody could fall in love with."

New Musical Express reviewed it; "The Stranglers are the great exiles of rock 'n' roll, and for some time now they've been making records that are both dispirited and resentful. That said, I still believe there is a place in our hearts for their curious blend of pessimism and romanticism. At times the sheer sense of fatigue and indifference in their music is almost cathartic. 'La Folie' — 'Madness' — is an uncomfortable, frequently unhappy jumble of snarls and sighs, but it shows that the group's obstinate despair can still manifest itself in both brash, hubristic satire and bleak, heart-sick melancholy. The stark but Byrne-ish and bellicose 'Let Me Introduce You To The Family' and the strident, self-reflective 'Man They Love To Hate' prove that the group can progress musically without compromising the essential misanthropy. For once, Dave Greenfield's keyboards work up to something more than distractive asides. Similarly, Cornwell's strange compassion is newly illuminated by the moving 'Tramp', with lines such as: 'A lost woman…'. Here The Stranglers are actually making the effort to make attractive music. I should stress that these are exceptions. For one convincingly angry success like 'Let Me Introduce You To The Family' there are three or four sombre and pretentious failures: the low-key, throwaway offensive — (almost a case of token male chauvinism!) — of 'Non Stop', a decidedly unbaroque vignette of a nun's repressed love, a schoolboy prank like 'Pin Up', or the chronically weary 'Ain't Nothin' To It', The Stranglers at their stalest ever."

"The most exasperating thing about the band is the lack of intelligence in the actual sound of the music. Where once Jean-Jacques Burnel's grunting bass and Greenfield's second-hand Manzarek organ doodling were hallmarks of punk bloody-mindedness, all four members now play as if they simply weren't interested, Burnel's bass sinks yet further back into the cleavage of Jet Black's zero degree beat, and Cornwell's guitar is all but lost in the fray. *La Folie*'s production is unnecessarily full — if one felt that they had even thought about economising somewhere that might be forgivable. The most impressive thing on the LP is 'La Folie' itself, sung in original François don't you know. It's high romanticism with a few strings — or at any rate Mellotrons — attached, but there's no swooning victory of love here. The song is a dirge about madness, a sad lament sung in a most deadpan tone with high, craning guitar, overbearing keyboards, and lines like 'Et si parfois l'on fait des confessions…'. It is at such unhappy, religious moments as these that The Stranglers' dark vision begins to shine."

Sounds reviewed it in December 1981; "Doggedly, almost despairingly, *La Folie* is a rock album. You know the score, the old ideas being painfully re-dredged in an attempt to make them sound new. And all the way through *La Folie* the yearning honesty is the desire to split up. Yes, a death rock album. The Stranglers were always too limited in scope and musical ideas to endure beyond the period when we were all punky and willing to have a good crack with them, the big nasty men of punk. They had a sort of Indian summer with *The Raven* but *La Folie*, like the awful *Meninblack*, reveals that the game is up. Strangled, you might say. It's mostly Hugh this time. He's given free rein for his predictable, again rather limited Honours Degree (un)penetrating "insight" to roam the corridors of Love. Disastrously, there are no tunes, not one on show. So it's a kind of cornball solo album with J.J. popping up only at the close for (the surprise!) a French love song. This is scarcely innovatory, never mind Hons Degree stuff."

"It's embarrassingly predictable. Titles give it away, like 'Non Stop' (about, Jesus, a nun — get it?), 'Pin Up' (about Marilyn — need I say more?) or 'It Only Takes Two To Tango' (about Nuclear Holocaust. I'm sure you're dying to hear that). The non-tunes of course rely on the subject matter, which reflect glaringly on the above. Which makes for a very odd stew indeed. As if it matters still, of course, the Strangleresque view of love is (again) doggedly one-sided. They even pen a paean to the tramp, literally a dosser. Surely this is taking love of men to its limit? Women? They are little toys and mostly to blame. It is a very cowardly base to start from. Not to say again revealing how in their senility The Stranglers, like all good old fellows, are shown to be really very old-fashionedly

English. They stand for traditional values — for rock as much as for the status quo in England. Indeed for this very reason they might still stand tall beside the likes of the conservative Exploited. Needless to say *La Folie* in its crippling weakness is shatteringly devoid of one element: love. I trust the next schedule met will reveal a suitably self-destruct concept at the end of the dream."

When *Record Mirror* reviewed *La Folie*, although they didn't speak highly of it, they were not overtly disparaging of it. Some of the staff behind this UK music paper were known to be good allies of The Stranglers. One would hope that this alone didn't inform the content of the review but still, it could be a factor: "Down in the morgue, children, you can see the body of The Stranglers who were given more than enough rope. Long dead, some say; but the fingers are twitching from under the shroud. They hold a new album and roses once again mix with the smell of blood. The tell-tale human heart is their theme and an anatomical sketch of such adorns the inside cover. The album vaguely deals with the victims and users of the stupidity the heart can cause. In other words *La Folie* is the madness of love, fine, off-centre idea from a band who after their first album lost their way and became a stagnant pool of self-important dirges. Under suspicion of fraud, *La Folie* stretches out in search of those early shadows. The track on the album 'Non Stop' brings the busy organ of Dave Greenfield and a one-tone voice in familiar Stranglers style but is spoilt by stupid lyrics, totally irrelevant and almost childish, in their nature of planned provocation. The same applies to 'Tramp' which scares heavily with superbly crafted music but 'The Man They Love To Hate' yields the best lines on the album. 'His father was a fighter and he practised on his son...'. Such is the between-the-eyes stuff I've missed."

"Side two twists and turns from the hackneyed subject of American and Russian chaps who could destroy us all.

'Golden Brown' has a gentle harpsichord lulling behind images of tanned dream girls travelling down the sand of the mind. Squeeze will listen with interest. Deep organ chords with the clean guitar and bass of the last, and title track... just works, despite the pretentious use of French lyrics. This is a cool slice of European darkness. The sordid puritan feel and blackness of the heart coming across even if you don't get the words. *La Folie* is at most, a reasonable follow up to *Rattus* and, at least a returned attention after the muddy slumbers of their last album. The morgue looks almost inviting."

It certainly wasn't all doom and gloom on the review front. *Smash Hits* gave *La Folie* an eight out of ten whilst stating; "An unexpected pleasure. The band have dropped their bully-boy tone and replaced it with a delicacy and lightness of touch that I thought I'd never hear from the hectoring Meninblack. The title, which refers to the whole madness of human life, is a strict guide to the record's contents — love, the family and the mental warps they can produce. For once, a sharp intelligence has been wrapped around The Stranglers' loudly held opinions."

In February 1982 — although a bit late to the party — the *Cumberland Evening News* and *Star Carlisle* reviewed *La Folie* under the heading of a "Non Stop Classic"; "From the opening Farfisa beat of 'Non Stop' to the final notes of the title track, *La Folie* is a classic. And it's only February. The Stranglers have found you don't need to throw everything plus the kitchen sink into an arrangement to make effective statements. There's an economy of style I first noticed on 'Duchess' and the mood is closer to solo Lou Reed at times to The Doors, who were always a strong influence. If you love 'Golden Brown', the hit single, that recalls Dave Brubeck and Gerry Marsden in one shot, then you'll be pleased to hear that every track is equally matchless. I noted in particular how Hugh Cornwell's solo sneaks up from behind and makes use of a guitar tone most musicians would dismiss as old-fashioned. Dave Greenfield is, of course, superb on keyboards, but the power of The Stranglers would not be the same without Jean-Jacques Burnel and Jet Black. I've a feeling that only The Jam will stand any chance of topping this disc before next January."

It wasn't until March 1982 that *Trouser Press* reviewed *La Folie* but nevertheless, it was a positive review that picked up on some of the excellent, finer points of the album: "Want to feel prematurely old? This, if you can believe it, is The Stranglers' seventh British album. While most alumni of the '77 punk explosion are long forgotten, The Stranglers continue to pump out albums (both band and solo) and singles. *La Folie* reassures and reasserts: The Stranglers are not only going strong, they're better than ever. The Stranglers' early records succeeded in direct proportion to their venom. The group pushed against the limits of cynicism and bile until they seemed in danger of self-parody. Starting with the catchy pop of 'Duchess' though, Stranglers songs have balanced the nice with the sleazy, the obscure with the easy. Since their discovery that gruff melodies and spat-out vocals aren't the only way to deliver serious lyrics, The Stranglers have been exploring more accessible settings for their satire and political commentary. The illustrations accompanying *La Folie*'s lyrics on the inner sleeve telegraph the punchlines in a way the songs themselves scarcely imitate. 'Everybody Loves You When You're Dead' doesn't seem about anyone in particular, except the pictures of Che Guevara and John Lennon clarify its intent. For the completely innocuous 'It Only Takes Two To Tango' we get a doctored photo of a waltzing Reagan and Brezhnev. The Stranglers now use the deceptively simple music to make their statements. Very little of their old heaviness remains, except in the sarcastic lyrics. You have to pay a little more attention to what they're doing and saying but — in *La Folie*'s case — the approach adds depth to a fine album from a maturing band."

The reviewer made excellent reference to the artwork

included with the LP. It is certainly one of those albums where the pleasure in listening to it can be enhanced by engaging with what's on the packaging. Also, an excellent point is made about how The Stranglers had progressed since their so-called punk days of 1977. Not to be disparaging of for example, the Sex Pistols or The Ramones, but by 1981, musically, The Stranglers had come into their own in a way that many of the groups that they were compared to at the start of the tenure, hadn't. One of the key strengths of *La Folie* is that it showcased what The Stranglers were capable of musically. Of course, their earlier albums are not without merit (far from it!) but commercially, the success of even just 'Golden Brown' as a single and the way in which it is such a well-known song in the mainstream today, just goes to show that *La Folie* signified a peak for The Stranglers that they hadn't quite reached in the same way with any of their earlier albums.

As is the case with all of The Stranglers' albums up to and including *La Folie*, it could be said that to get the most out of the music, it is worth knowing about the context of the subjects that the band are referring to. This is especially the case on *La Folie* with not just the way in which the band explored themes of love but in references to subjects that aren't as well known such as Milton Mezzrow and Issei Sagawa. Can *La Folie* be enjoyed without such knowledge? Absolutely! But one of the fascinating things about the album is that there are so many layers to it — it's really just a question of how keen a listener may be to delve.

International Musician & Recording World considered in November 1982; "The Stranglers have endured the rigours and perils of the industry without sacrificing their originality. Many bands are compelled, for various reasons, to change course, make concessions or even sell out all together in pursuit of that most elusive of ambitions — the record deal. Not so with The Stranglers. They have maintained their unique identity and have flatly refused to be manipulated by their critics and adverse publicity. Recently, however, even their closest followers have noticed what appears to be an amount of mellowing to the band — at least in the music if not in attitude... The Stranglers have never been a particularly easy band to pin down. They have been landed with a somewhat unfortunate reputation which is probably as much a product of fertile imaginations as it is actual case incidents. Nevertheless, if it came to the crunch, you would feel obliged to categorise them as anti-heroes rather than outright villains. Whether you like them or not, you can't deny that they're certainly an intriguing bunch of characters who have come up with a most interesting sound and style... Their material seems to be edging toward a more subtle approach... What many are misinterpreting to be a sell out is, in fact, a natural development of the band — a maturing if you like. Besides, the progression is evident in other areas too if one listens carefully. Areas like musicianship and lyrical content. If anything, far from losing their grip, the band are gathering momentum."

Chapter Three

Touring

In November 1981, *Record Mirror* asked; "What would it mean if *La Folie* flopped? Is The Stranglers' future largely dependent on the success of this album?" Cornwell's reply was a pragmatic one: "I don't think it's down to albums, it's down to tours. If we played in Britain and nobody came to see us — then I think that would be more indicative that not many people are buying our records. *Meninblack* sold, I think, 50,000 copies. Well, if there's 50,000 people still in the country who want to buy our records then I can't think that we've flopped. I was disappointed with 'Who Wants The World?' because I really thought it was the best single we'd ever made. It was really well produced, it had a good sound. I really like the song, and I think we were amazed that it didn't go well when it was released. But there you go, life's full of surprises."

The number of songs from *La Folie* that featured on the tour that followed its release were a clear indicator of The Stranglers' satisfaction with them. In October 1981 Jet Black told the *Liverpool Echo*; "We are rampant at the moment. Like mad dogs — just can't wait for the tour to get going."

The tour was a relatively short one that spanned either side of Christmas 1981. Commencing on 11th November just two days after the album's release, it ran up to and including 8th February 1982. It was during this period of touring that 'Golden Brown' was successfully climbing the UK singles chart.

In terms of how the songs translated from album to stage, Burnel told *Black & White* in 1982; "It's never exactly the same.

It's loyal to the feeling if it's not to the sound. But nothing we create in the studio is impossible to reproduce. We never use tapes as most of our contemporaries do. We just have a genius that does everything — D. Greenfield." (Notably, although on record, 'Golden Brown' features an actual harpsichord, on stage Greenfield used a synthesiser to play that part).

Greenfield told *Strangled* in 1982; "As far as stage work is concerned I like things that are a challenge to play. We always play faster live than we do when recording or writing so if I write something — a passage or a riff or whatever — in a song and it's difficult, I make it as hard as I can. Then when we come to play it live it speeds up so much it's a challenge and I really enjoy that."

Member of the London City Ballet, Anastasia Brown choreographed and danced to 'Waltzinblack' along with other dancers. Their performances were staged immediately prior to The Stranglers taking the stage at both the Hammersmith Palais and at the Rainbow Theatre in 1981.

The Stranglers used some visuals on the tour albeit relatively primitive ones (including the word "Folie" spelt out with humans — thanks to help from the support act — displaying the letters).

When asked if he felt whether The Stranglers would use video on stage as part of their set, Cornwell told *Strangled* in 1981; "When you experience life, unless you are blind or deaf, you get a mixture of all the senses picking up at the same time. So ideally you should be able to experience something which takes into account all of those senses, so obviously we will work — I think the whole of Western art is working — towards a total experience. But it's quite frightening, that, because once you can create that people will want to live in an artificial world all the time — it will just be like a drug... It could be misused. I imagine you could get tremendous propaganda value from a three-dimensional, five-sense attack on someone. I'm sure someone's going to misuse it one day."

Bootleg audio exists of the performance that took place at the Hammersmith Palais on 17th November 1981. The Stranglers played numbers from *La Folie*. It's a likelihood that at this point, not everyone in the audience was familiar with the songs and this may have seemed like the case all the more in view of the musical complexity of them. Nevertheless, 'The Man They Love To Hate', 'Let Me Introduce You To The Family', 'Non Stop' and 'Tramp' are played with an infectious extent of energy and conviction. Apparently, this performance was filmed by a French TV crew but whether or not the footage still exists or indeed whether it will ever get to see the light of day now is anyone's guess.

In November 1981 under the heading of "Surprises From The Stranglers" the *Stapleford & Sandiacre News* reported; "After slightly losing their way following their first album, The Stranglers are now back with a bang and Nottingham's Rock City was treated to a memorable show on Friday. Noted for being unpredictable and for not playing old numbers crowds request, the Meninblack pulled out a few surprises when they played 'Bring On The Nubiles' and 'I Feel Like A Wog' from the *No More Heroes* album and 'Threatened' from *Black And White*. The numbers they played from their new album *La Folie* were excellent, especially 'Golden Brown' and 'Let Me Introduce You To The Family' — which has been released on the band's latest single. Dave Greenfield had problems with his keyboards half-way through 'Thrown Away' but Hugh Cornwell kept the crowd happy with jokes and chat. 'Thrown Away' was again interrupted when Jean-Jacques Burnel threatened one person in the crowd who had been harassing him throughout and the band went straight into an explosive version of 'Tank'. 'Who Wants The World?' and 'Nuclear Device' kept the audience moving and the majestic 'Duchess', the band's only major hit other than 'No More Heroes' was played as a second encore before a late finish with 'The Raven'. First on stage were the uninspiring French band Taxi Girl, who are currently popular in their own country but were, to me, extremely silly and only mildly entertaining."

Some comments from the reviewer suggest that at an absolute maximum, they may have only been a casual fan of The Stranglers. For of course, it wasn't just the band's first album that was a success and indeed, they had many more successes with singles than just 'No More Heroes'. Also, as The Stranglers had often stipulated, they themselves were not — as the reviewer calls them — the Meninblack. Nevertheless, the review comes across as fair and candid. Positive reviews from journalists who don't come with a strong bias towards a band are perhaps sometimes worth that little bit more in an instance like this.

The first thing that fans heard from *La Folie* was the track 'Let Me Introduce You To The Family', released just ahead of the album. The B-side was the non-album track 'Vietnamerica'.

Although the label didn't say "from the forthcoming album…" at least the back cover advertised the upcoming La Folie tour. Interestingly the Italian release of this single had the same back sleeve with UK tour dates!

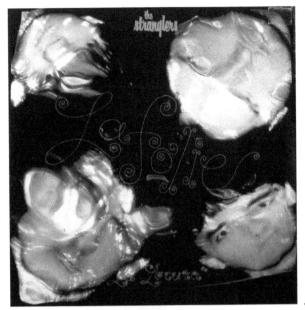

Spain

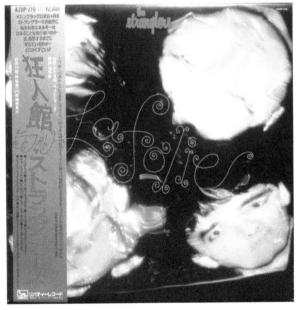

Japan

There wasn't really anything in the way of cover variations except the Spanish version had the French title also in Spanish. The Japanese version came with the ubiquitous wrap-around obi with the album information translated for the consumers.

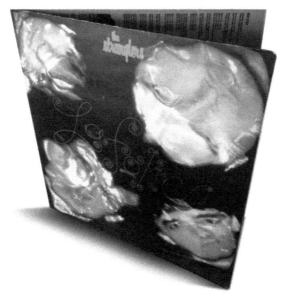

Although the album was released in a single sleeve with a printed inner sleeve, Zimbabwe released it as a gatefold by utilising the inner sleeve artwork.

UK

France

Portugal

There were variations on the artwork in the popular cassette format to accommodate the change from square to rectangular form.

The second single released from the album proved to be the winning formula. Sadly the sleeve design wasn't much to write home about although at least the Spanish had the title in both languages, whilst in Germany it was also released as a 12" single.

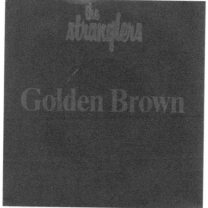

UK

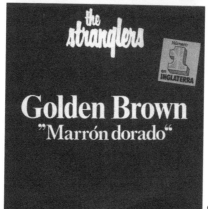

Spain

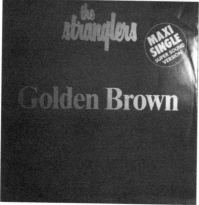

Germany

UK

France

Portugal

South Africa

DJ single UK

Single UK

The third single culled from the album was the title track, sung in French by Jean-Jacques. The DJ promo copies were an edited version for radio play and although commercial releases claimed to be shorter than the LP version, it was in fact the full version.

Live at the Hammersmith Odeon '82

THEARCHIVESERIES

The Hammersmith Odeon gig from the tour was recorded by the BBC and pressed up on vinyl for one radio broadcast. It was later released on CD by EMI.

The setlist for the gig performed at Edinburgh Playhouse on 22nd November is demonstrative of how even though The Stranglers were clearly pleased with *La Folie*, it wasn't to the extent that they had ditched material from their previous albums:

1. Intro
2. Non Stop
3. Threatened
4. Just Like Nothing On Earth
5. Second Coming
6. The Man They Love To Hate
7. Meninblack
8. Who Wants The World?
9. Baroque Bordello
10. Golden Brown
11. Tramp
12. Thrown Away
13. Tank
14. I Feel Like A Wog
15. Let Me Introduce You To The Family
16. Nuclear Device
17. Genetix
18. Bring On The Nubiles (Cocktail Version)
19. Bring On The Nubiles
20. Duchess
21. The Raven

The Stranglers - *La Folie*: In-depth

On 23rd January 1982, The Stranglers played at Leicester University. The audio was recorded and distributed as a bootleg and thank goodness it was! It features some excellent versions of the songs from *La Folie*. A great representation of what The Stranglers sounded like live at this stage in their tenure (also — forgiving the fact that many bootleg recordings may not feature songs in the order in which they were played — notice how the setlist on the La Folie tour wasn't a rigid one; it varied quite a lot from one gig to the next):

1. Intro
2. Down In The Sewer
3. Just Like Nothing On Earth
4. Second Coming
5. Non Stop
6. The Man They Love To Hate
7. Who Wants The World?
8. Baroque Bordello
9. Golden Brown
10. How To Find True Love And Happiness In The Present Day
11. Thrown Away
12. Tank
13. Let Me Introduce You To The Family
14. Tramp
15. The Raven

The Stranglers played at Brighton's Top Rank Suite on 25th January 1982. The bootleg of this performance shows, yet again, a band very much at the top of their game.

1. Intro
2. Down In The Sewer
3. Just Like Nothing On Earth
4. Second Coming
5. Non Stop
6. The Man They Love To Hate
7. Who Wants The World?
8. Baroque Bordello
9. Golden Brown
10. How To Find True Love And Happiness In The Present Day
11. Thrown Away
12. Tank
13. Let Me Introduce You To The Family
14. Tramp
15. The Raven
16. Encore break
17. Announcement
18. Nuclear Device
19. Genetix

Just three days later when The Stranglers played at Hemel Hempstead Pavilion on 28th January, a different setlist was offered:

1. Intro
2. Down In The Sewer
3. Second Coming
4. Non Stop
5. The Man They Love To Hate
6. Who Wants The World?
7. Baroque Bordello
8. Golden Brown
9. How To Find True Love And Happiness In The Present Day
10. Duchess
11. Tank
12. Let Me Introduce You To The Family
13. Tramp
14. The Raven
15. Nuclear Device
16. Genetix

The gig was reviewed under the heading of "Home Come The Heroes"; "After years of touring and a constant battle to reach the very top, The Stranglers have finally broken the boundary with just one single, 'Golden Brown' and stumbled upon a whole new audience. On their pre-Christmas tour before their recent success they were dismissed as "punk revivalists" drifting along the same type of tunes they were playing back in the 'Peaches' and 'No More Heroes' era. Suddenly, they deliver a record whose sound is virtually unclassifiable (psychedelic revival?) and everyone wants to know them. They're hip again. The concert was formulated with material mostly from their last two albums but a powerful version of 'Down In The Sewer' opened up the performance, with chanting for the band from the under-eighteens. Half of the old fans present, pogo-danced throughout the night. The rest stood in the balcony and listened. The whole set was exciting, and very tight, ploughing through at great speed. Hugh's vocals have become more distinct and listenable. J.J. provided rapid, strong bass lines and with eyes on his guitar, appeared in his usual, sultry trance-like pose. Most of the songs were uplifted by excellent keyboard additions from Dave Greenfield. The only time the show slowed down was for 'Golden Brown', where the whole crowd clapped and swayed to the tune (unforeseen!), with another huge cheer when they finished it. For the encore, the most powerful song of the night, they played 'Nuclear Device'. It's hard to believe that it's taken The Stranglers four years to reach the height of popularity — having stumbled upon it at that. By the time they return to Bristol, at the end of this tour, they'll be heroes for sure. As for the rest of us it will be interesting to see if they continue their success by making commercial records. But they'll always be great, live."

When The Stranglers played at the Oasis in Swindon on 30th January, such was the interest in the gig that hundreds who wanted to be in the audience were unable to get a ticket. Unsurprising really in view of how the band were enjoying the chart success of 'Golden Brown' around that time. Also, some venues had already sold a lot of tickets even before 'Golden Brown' became a factor in the demand for them. The Swindon gig made the news due to a spitting incident — spitting was all part of it for The Stranglers when they started out but on this occasion, they'd had enough of it.

Under the headline of "Spitting Fan Who Had To Bare It!" the gig was reviewed in Swindon's *Evening Advertiser*; "Pop group The Stranglers had a special way of dealing with spitting punk fans. They were showered with spit at the start of their sell-out Swindon show on Saturday. So they hauled one of the offenders onto the stage — and pulled down his trousers and pants. And in front of 1,500 fans, they administered a jolly good spanking. The foul spitting — which was supposed to be a way of showing appreciation — stopped immediately. A Stranglers spokesman said the group, not unnaturally, hated being spat at. He said: 'They often have to make an example of someone — and this method seems to work best.' Hundreds of fans were turned away from The Oasis before the show. Manager Mr Roland Honeybunn said they could have almost sold the show twice. A plate glass door valued at around £200 was smashed as fans attempted to break in before the concert. The door was shattered as youngsters struggled with bouncers."

Further commentary on the gig was printed in the same paper a few days later; "The Stranglers were plunging through 'Down In The Sewer' when the spitting started. Cornwell, a swarthy type, isn't a man to be spat at. Hauling a particularly vociferous and then amazed offender to the stage, Cornwell and roadies exacted punishment. They whipped off the blighter's strides and administered a jolly good thwacking. Three thousand eyes watched gleefully. The struggling, squealing punk was red cheeked with embarrassment. An example had been made — and the vile spitting immediately ceased. It was the highlight of the sold-out Swindon Oasis show on Saturday; a good, if not particularly great gig in which the Meninblack merged their doom-laden attack of yore with glowing new-found maturity."

"It was their first Swindon show since a memorably sparsely attended affair in '77. But even they, The Stranglers, were the odd-men-out in the so-called new wave explosion. They coincided, rather than contributed to punk. When spiky brats were preaching anarchy and rebellion, The Stranglers were dwelling on the darker, gloomier, seedier side of life. They were labelled sexist (with some justification). It killed them off in the eyes of the make 'em break 'em pop press. But now a hit single. An album of intermittent excellence. The

Stranglers are back in (big) business. Dave Greenfield's thickly swirling keyboards are still the backbone to the group's quasi-Doors sound. He is nestled behind a battery of keyboards in a black-clad tower. Cornwell and Burnel are below. Guitars slung low, the obvious (focal) and vocal points. Grim-faced Jet Black thumps dourly amidst the black backdrop. There is invariably a splatter of ugly pomp and grandeur about the music. Songs are either punchy or insinuating. But they are often overlong. They played 'Nuclear Device'. 'The best bloody reason in the world for writing a song' says Cornwell. 'Golden Brown' wafted deliciously across the hushed auditorium. It is a haunting, shimmering piece which refreshingly eschews the format structure of a hit single and still made it to the top."

Of the spitting/spanking incident, *The Daily Mirror* reported in February 1982; "The Stranglers, who have a new "gentle" image, were playing at a leisure centre in Swindon, Wilts. The manager there, Roland Honeybunn, said yesterday: 'there were dozens of punks at the front of the audience, spitting at the group as they played. Apparently it's their way of showing they like someone. But the group didn't like being on the receiving end. After the spanking they told the crowd, 'We come here to play and we want you to listen.' It did the trick. The spitting stopped immediately.' A spokesman for the group, whose love song 'Golden Brown' is currently at number three in the charts, said, 'They hated being spat at, even though the fans were only showing approval. They decided to make an example of one of the ringleaders and it seemed to work'."

Perhaps by 1982, there was a disparity between what The Stranglers wanted to do musically and the audience (well, some of them!) that they were still attracting; ones that seemingly had expectations for the same aggression and rioting to be present as had been case in the band's earlier days.

Not long after the La Folie tour, a fan wrote to *Strangled* in 1982; "I want to take this opportunity to get something off my chest. The Stranglers were unfortunate to come into being at the time when the "punk rock" craze swept the earth. Whilst I've nothing to say against punk rock (but nothing to say for it) The Stranglers have NEVER been punk rockers. Punk rock is defined in the dictionary as 'type of pop music involving outrage and shock effects.' Fair enough, the band may have produced a couple of mildly outrageous songs in the past, but when I hear the likes of 'Golden Brown' and 'Strange Little Girl' and last — but definitely not least — the amazingly brilliant 'Cruel Garden', it angers, upsets and frustrates me to see some idiots walking around the streets, wearing jackets emblazoned with Anti-Nowhere League, Dead Kennedys AND The Stranglers. This is nothing short of blasphemy. I'm not saying it's wrong to like the aforementioned groups as well as The Stranglers, of course it isn't, but I do think it's wrong to associate them with The Stranglers. The Stranglers have changed and I think some of the fans will have to accept that fact. To be quite honest, I'm dreading the next Stranglers gig, where, again, I'll find myself surrounded by people with these offensive jackets, gobbing everywhere and probably wondering 'Whatever happened to…?'"

Cornwell told *Strangled* in 1981; "I think rock audiences are a very specific, specialised group of people. They're either into a band's music who they're going to see, or they've heard about it, or they're into music in general. Right now I think you could say that everyone in their life has been to see a film at a cinema, but not everyone has been to a rock concert."

Spitting incidents aside, the setlist for Swindon was enough to whet anyone's appetite:

1. Down In The Sewer
2. Just Like Nothing On Earth
3. Second Coming
4. Non Stop
5. The Man They Love To Hate

6. Who Wants The World?
7. Baroque Bordello
8. Golden Brown
9. How To Find True Love And Happiness In The Present Day
10. Duchess
11. Tank
12. Let Me Introduce You To The Family
13. Tramp
14. The Raven
15. Nuclear Device
16. Genetix

Perhaps one of the strongest bootleg recordings from the La Folie tour is that from the Ipswich Gaumont gig on 5th February. The audio was released on an LP titled *The Men They Love To Hate*. The sound quality is excellent but it's plausible that it's not the full set from that night. The recording features just the following:

1. Intro
2. Down In The Sewer
3. Just Like Nothing On Earth
4. Second Coming
5. Non Stop
6. The Man They Love To Hate
7. Golden Brown
8. How To Find True Love And Happiness In The Present Day
9. Tank
10. Let Me Introduce You To The Family
11. Tramp
12. The Raven
13. Nuclear Device

When the La Folie tour was announced, there was disappointment for some. Clearly, despite everything that had happened before, The Stranglers were still in demand. The group's absence was felt in Reading. In August 1981, the *Reading Evening Post* complained that the band "are also on the road in November, calling at Hammersmith Palais on 17th" and the fact that whilst not playing in Reading, they would be "playing other towns as varied as Cardiff and Brighton" and that it served to highlight "the lack of facilities in the town".

On the other hand, there were some venues that turned down The Stranglers' offer to make an appearance — even in the name of charity! *Strangled* reported in 1982; "The band offered to play a benefit gig for Cambridge Woman's Aid. The offer was refused in a letter which stated that 'I thought that I had made it clear when you first mentioned the possibility that the group were not suitable from our point of view and that we did not wish to be associated with them in view of their previous exploitation of women as expressed in lyrics. I am sorry if this misunderstanding has caused you any inconvenience'."

Rightly or wrongly, it is clear that many still associated The Stranglers with how they may have viewed the band in the late seventies. Then again though, did the release of *La Folie* signify a change of attitude within the band? Well, that's an incredibly difficult question to answer on the basis that it depends on whether the band were truly sexist in the first place! Again, it's all incredibly subject to opinion and interpretation based on a) the views of any individual and b) what their values are in line with those that The Stranglers may or may not have been trying to promote on that front (if anything!).

Some in the media still refused to make time for The Stranglers based on the band's behaviour in the earlier days of their career. According to *Strangled* magazine in 1982, one fan received this letter in response to an enquiry:

The reason you have not seen The Stranglers on The Old Grey Whistle Test *is because a couple of years back I mounted a* Rock Goes To College *programme with the band from Guildford University, and half-way through the second number the band walked off stage refusing to continue with the recording. Apart from the fact that this was a costly occurrence for the BBC in that a whole Outside Broadcast Unit had to be made available with no end product, it also denied another band the opportunity of recording a concert programme for television. I therefore feel somewhat disinclined to work with the band after this experience.*

> *Yours sincerely*
> *Michael Appleton*
> *Producer,* The Old Grey Whistle Test.

Of course, The Stranglers had their reasons for having walked off. Mainly that, as Cornwell put it; "We had a lack of control over the distribution of the tickets… our real fans from the town of Guildford would feel that we had actively excluded them from the gig, especially since we were prevented from playing any other venue in Guildford." (Students at the university had been given priority to get hold of tickets for the performance). Note that not the entire BBC shunned The Stranglers, just *The Old Grey Whistle Test.*

By 1982, The Stranglers had remained consistent in their support of CND, the Prisoners' Rights movement and other pressure groups. They were keen not to promote a subscription to any particular ideology though. Burnel said, "I find the idea of left and right rather absurd, that particular division. A lot of people think we're fascists 'cos direct action — like hitting someone — is meant to be fascist because it's not done by committee. Action seems to have been sewn up by the right."

True to their beliefs, The Stranglers played at the No Nukes

Festival in Utrecht on 9th April 1982. The setlist was:

1. Intro
2. Down In The Sewer,
3. Just Like Nothing On Earth
4. Second Coming
5. Non Stop
6. The Man They Love To Hate
7. Who Wants The World?
8. Baroque Bordello
9. Golden Brown
10. How To Find True Love And Happiness In The Present Day
11. Tank
12. Let Me Introduce You To The Family
13. Tramp
14. The Raven
15. Nuclear Device
16. Genetix
17. La Folie

Cornwell told *New Musical Express* in 1982; "We played a No Nukes gig in Utrecht — I think it was the biggest indoor event in Holland ever, around 30,000 people. They weren't just Dutch, they were French, Belgian, German, Swiss — all you have to do is find an issue like that which goes right across the board. There's nothing wrong in being proud of being English, French or whatever as long as you realise that there are people who have the right to be proud of what they are. One thing I was very pissed off about was that the anti-nuke compilation album, *Life In The European Theatre*, wasn't a million seller. None of the audience I spoke to on our European tour had even heard of it."

Chapter Four

Legacy

It could be said that the release and success of *La Folie* empowered The Stranglers with the perfect opportunity to get away from the weird and heavy image they had acquired as a result of the *Meninblack* album. In November 1981, *Record Mirror* asked, "Did you find yourselves being closeted by the *Meninblack* album? That was the first time that it seemed The Stranglers had suddenly acquired some kind of image." Cornwell's response: "I think we felt a bit claustrophobic in that whole thing. All the bad luck we were having, and all the calamities — it was a period of catastrophes for us and I think we felt the more that happened, the more it was going to happen — you get very fatalistic about that sort of situation. I was very glad that with *La Folie* we started breaking out of that. It feels like a breath of fresh air — and I think the music reflects it as well." When asked if it was difficult to drop the whole Meninblack concept, Cornwell said; "No, we'd just had enough of it. We had enough of the sombre, ominous, heaviness about it. It's a very fascinating topic, but I don't know whether it's necessary to bore the pants off people with it."

Perhaps, as with a lot of The Stranglers' music, people had taken the *Meninblack* album too seriously in how it informed their perception of the band. Cornwell said in the same interview; "There's two ways of looking at a lot of the stuff we write about. You can either look at it totally directly and you get freaked out and horrified, or you can see that there's a bit of a chuckle in there and have a laugh with us. That's been a lot of the problem about being misunderstood and people getting upset by us."

When asked if this was supposed to be the case with the *Meninblack* album, Cornwell replied; "A lot of the ideas on it were, yes. 'Just like Nothing On Earth' was very tongue in cheek. It was about the popular side of UFO spotting. It was drawing a correlation between UFO spotting and people in cars at night. It just seems that the two have gone hand in hand. I mean, 'Waltz In Black', how can anyone take the laughing on that seriously?"

Still though, the opportunity had been there to indulge their curiosities and there were moments in which some members of the band had been given the chance to represent their interests on a theme. Cornwell told BBC Radio in January 1983; "Jet and I spent about three months last year working on a documentary film for BBC West, which unfortunately has never been seen outside of that area. They showed it on a programme called *RPM*, which just goes out as a local regional arts programme. They gave us fifteen minutes of time and they said make anything you want. So Jet and I started researching the colour black. We thought it's about time. We wanted to find out more about it. We thought great, we can make a film about it. So we made a little documentary about the colour black, and it was amazing what we unearthed."

"We found out about people's reaction to the colour black and why they react to it. People feel threatened by it. But then a clergyman told us that priests wear black because it's a sober colour and the person who wears it is predictable; it's conservative and it shows no rank. Zorro is a good guy and Dracula is a bad guy yet they both wear black and they are symbolised by black. Then you've got the Nazis and Oswald Mosley's Blackshirts using it to sort of instil people with fear. There's this constant link with authority; judges always wear black and the police wear black. After doing this research we said well, we want to do a one hour film on it, and they said 'no way'. It's fascinating; it's a non-colour. It's not in the spectrum. It's sort of all the other things that aren't seen with the naked eye."

"Of all those people and all those contradictions, human nature is totally baffled by black. It just doesn't understand it and it leads to confusion, basically. We're more interested in a general way. Why we wear black is because we're fed up with people planting us with images. When we started, journalists would say 'What's your image boys? What are you going from?' We said 'We have no image. Why do you have to have an image? We play music and we are as we are.' And they don't like it. They say, 'Right, well, in that case, we're going to give you an image okay? You're punks. Right?' And so us wearing black is trying to say we have no image. It's just, a colour, well, a non-colour."

And indeed, an image can serve as either a blessing or a curse. Regarding how many people were saying that *La Folie* sounded so different to The Stranglers' previous work, Cornwell told the BBC in 1982; "That's why it's getting played on the radio, because they don't realise it's us."

Whilst it *is* a popular narrative to regard *La Folie* as the album that saved The Stranglers' career commercially, it is vital not to dismiss *The Meninblack* as a complete disaster; it is far from it! Burnel said of the album in later years; "I'm very fond of *The Meninblack* because it's so completely off-the-wall. Obviously it suffers from the fact that it was done by The Stranglers, and so got viewed negatively. It was never regarded as an art album, because people just didn't see us in that light, apart from *Billboard*'s reviewer who said it was a work of genius. If you're going out having punch-ups, being physical savages, you're not allowed to have intellectual pretensions. But we had a foot in both camps, really. Maybe it needs to be rehabilitated, yeah. If people can survive listening to the whole of it, it might be recognised. It certainly came from another place. Fuck knows where that place is."

Due to The Stranglers' commercial success with *La Folie* (and indeed, 'Golden Brown'), several record companies were keen to sign them once their contract with EMI came to an end. Virgin Records was considered a likely candidate but Epic Records (under the umbrella of parent company CBS) came in at the last minute and sealed the deal. Burnel recalled; "When we left EMI, everyone was after us. I remember going on Richard Branson's boat in London as he wanted to sign us to Virgin. We eventually plumped for CBS and they put a lot of money behind the release of *Feline*."

It's worth noting that the transition wasn't a completely smooth one. *Record Business* reported in April 1982; "A battle over recording contracts led The Stranglers to give High Court undertakings last week 'not to render services as recording artistes' to anyone other than EMI Records, pending a further court hearing set for early May. Romie Tager, counsel for EMI, told Mr Justice Vinelott that in December 1976 the group made a record contract with United Artists which was later assigned to EMI. Since February this year the group had been claiming that they were not bound by that agreement. This was disputed by EMI which had started an action against the four group members claiming more than £157,000 and injunctions to restrain the band from breaching its record contract. Since then, said Tager, EMI had been told The Stranglers had made a deal with someone else. 'That would be a gross breach of their obligations to EMI if the December 1976 agreement was still binding,' he said. EMI's claim for temporary injunctions against the four group members — Hugh Cornwell, David Greenfield, Brian Duffy (a.k.a. Jet Black) and Jean-Jacques Burnel — was adjourned until May 4th and the undertakings remain in force until then."

EMI was quick off the mark in getting their pound of

flesh with the release of the compilation album *The Collection 1977–1982* in August 1982. It was the first of many that EMI would release to exploit the material in the catalogue that was still controlled by them.

In late 1982, Cornwell told *New Musical Express* of The Stranglers' dynamic with EMI; "We both realised it wasn't working and we came to an agreement to leave. They really got us by mistake, when they took over United Artists, our original label."

Signing with Epic would see The Stranglers being able to enjoy full artistic freedom and in 1983 their first record released on the label was *Feline*. The album hosted the single 'European Female' which got to number nine in the UK. Influenced by European music and the first Stranglers album to feature acoustic guitars and Jet Black's extensive use of electronic drum kits, *Feline* represented another musical change in direction for the band.

The way in which *La Folie* was made went on to inform how The Stranglers worked on *Feline*. Cornwell said; "On *La Folie* there were three tracks — 'Golden Brown' ... 'La Folie' and 'How To Find True Love And Happiness In The Present Day' — that sort of pointed us away from what we had been doing. It was strange doing those tracks, because we'd never really attempted that quite minimalistic recording technique. And when we started writing for *Feline*, things were coming out the same way."

As had been the case with *La Folie*, The Stranglers had Steve Churchyard as engineer for the *Feline* sessions. He also helped them with the album's production. In addition, Tony Visconti was drafted in again for the final week to mix the tracks. In later years Burnel considered that working with The Stranglers gave Visconti's career a boost: "I remember picking Tony up from the airport and he was waxing lyrical about what we had done for his career. After his Bowie period his career had gone downhill and had been in the doldrums for a bit, and working on 'Golden Brown' had revived it. We'd helped get his name back up in lights."

On the yet-to-be released *Feline* album, it was reported in *International Musician & Recording World* in November 1982; "The latest album was made at IPC Studios in Brussels. Hugh was reluctant to say anything about the concept or the material and its release is not scheduled until early in the New Year. A single may be put out this side of Christmas, but as far as tour plans are concerned, there are no intentions to do any live work anywhere for the remainder of 1982. It is worth noting that Tony Visconti was invited in to give his opinion on the mixing of the new album. Tony, of course, was also involved with the production of 'Golden Brown' but Hugh was anxious to point out that the album itself was produced by The Stranglers in association with their engineer, Steve Churchyard."

Cornwell commented; "We invited Tony in to mix the tracks because we do appreciate a different opinion, coming in and hearing the stuff fresh after we've recorded it. We worked with him on the *La Folie* album and it worked so we kept the arrangement."

Clearly, what was achieved in the studio with *La Folie* was certainly something that The Stranglers wished to repeat — at least, in terms of the process — when it came to making *Feline*.

Feline got to number four in the UK and it helped to boost The Stranglers' career significantly in Europe.

Trouser Press reviewed *Feline* in May 1983; "Anyone who still associates The Stranglers with gutter rave-ups like 'London Lady' and 'Down In The Sewer' just hasn't listened to them in a while. Over the last few years the band has moved steadily away from the calculated gross-out and towards a much more subtle pop subversion. *Feline* is so appealing it's possibly insidious. Take 'Midnight Summer Dream' for example. After a romantic spindly keyboard solo from Dave Greenfield, bass, drums and acoustic guitar enter to accompany Hugh Cornwell's recitation — a dour reverie touching on right and wrong, appearance and illusion. These are hardly standard song topics, but a sinuous beat and seductive arrangement mask the philosophy. You're sucked into the tune before realising how disturbingly introspective it is. That's *Feline*'s modus operandi. 'It's A Small World' has a sing-songy verse, wandering organ and plaintive synthesised "strings" to mask vaguely threatening lyrics ('watch a flower die of thirst'). The snappy 'Ships That Pass In The Night' employs a jazzish major-seventh guitar progression and sustained "brass" textured keyboard tones in the service of sly sarcasm ('vote for a politician as a ship to pass in the night')."

"The songs on side two, with their European place names and shared theme of restlessness, are more clearly tied together than those on side one (The Stranglers are no strangers to conceptual albums, as *The Meninblack* has proved). 'Paradise', the album's loudest song, hammers home its message in a repeated refrain ('I don't think anyone's ever found paradise...'). But even in this relative stridency — a shouted (albeit not dominant) vocal and glaring lyric — is jarring only in present muted company. A couple of tracks make more obeisance to dance rock than others, yet an ominous vocal ('All Roads Lead To Rome') or free-floating keyboards and a swooping melody ('Blue Sister') undercut and lightheartedness. Behind its pretty exterior, *Feline* is ready to pounce. 'The European Female (In Celebration Of)', ostensibly a breathy love song, is the album's sole resting place (its cop from David Bowie's 'Station To Station' even introduces an element of humour). Beware the Bachian keyboard sextuplets on 'Let's Tango In Paris' like the rolling metre and crooning Cornwell on 'Golden Brown'. Like the siren to which the latter refers, The Stranglers now lure listeners instead of repelling them, but their goal of disquietude remains the same. *Feline* is an impressive, unclassifiable work from a band that's never cared much about identification labels."

Record Business reviewed *Feline* in January 1983; "The Stranglers' first Epic album suggests retrenchment of a kind rather than a continuation of previously indicated moves towards a wider record-buying public. Side one, featuring their unconvincing single 'European Female' is a dour, introspective effort. The reverse shows rather more promise with occasional signs of a desire to sing, but the approach remains low-key and oppressively doomy. Consumer reaction will be interesting, if difficult to assess up-front."

Later releases of *La Folie* on CD include additional songs, some of which are from the B-sides of the associated singles.

'Cruel Garden' is a beautiful instance of melodic jazz; a tribute to the guitarist, Jean Baptiste Reinhardt.

'Cocktail Nubiles' is a humorous, cabaret take on the earlier song, 'Bring On The Nubiles', as featured on *No More Heroes* in 1977.

There's 'Vietnamerica', which was the B-side to 'Let Me Introduce You To The Family'.

'Love 30', the B-side of 'Golden Brown' is an instrumental. *Strangled* reported in 1982; "The B-side of 'Golden Brown', 'Love 30', an instrumental number, was inspired by the controversial tennis playing of John McEnroe. In the background the sounds of a game of tennis in progress can be heard."

'You Hold The Key To My Love In Your Hands' was made during the recording of *La Folie* but it was felt that it didn't fit well with the rest of the material. The song didn't get its first release until 1999 when EMI included it on the compilation album, *Hits & Heroes*.

'Strange Little Girl' was The Stranglers' last single with EMI. It got to number seven in the UK — a strong position considering that EMI had rejected the song previously. It was included on *The Collection 1977–1982*, which peaked at number twelve. Although the album fell just shy of the top ten overall, The Stranglers were able to leave EMI on a high.

Smash Hits reviewed 'Strange Little Girl' in July 1982; "Dear me. 'Golden Brown' and now this. Even the nasty rough Stranglers have gone all mellow and soft in the middle. They're much better this way, actually, even though this one sounds suspiciously psychedelic. A hit, probably."

Considering that it had been written in 1974, it's interesting how the reviewer notes that 'Strange Little Girl' sounds a bit psychedelic. Does it sound *that* psychedelic though? Relatively speaking, seemingly not.

'Strange Little Girl' was composed in 1974 by Hugh Cornwell and Hans Wärmling. Wärmling played keyboards and guitar as a member of the band (yet to be called The Stranglers!). He left and was replaced by Dave Greenfield in 1975. In 1982, The Stranglers chose to go with the song as a single in the hopes that it would attract a similar audience to those who had supported 'Golden Brown'. The song mentions Cornwell's ex-girlfriend — the same one who is mentioned on 'Sometimes' on *Rattus Norvegicus*. The idea of 'Strange Little Girl' is that the woman went to live in a remote village. Also though, it is in homage to the French writer Alain-René Lesage and his novel *Gil Blas* (which is about social realism and the way in which unprotected children can be exploited).

New Musical Express considered in September 1982; "Amid the bright motes of fairydust caught floating in the spotlights of 1982's *Top Of The Pops*, the recurring shadow cast by the murky presence of The Stranglers has been one of the year's more bizarre chart events. But there it has been: one camera-cut away and a DJ's plastic smile away from the raging limbs of this week's chart sensation (is it a group? is it a dance troupe? is it a team of Moroccan tumblers?) and the old sewer rats are glowering out like the elder brother and his morose friends at a teenage birthday party. Even more freakish, instead of slugging out the mawkish sweaty thud that their customary reputation would demand, the quartet have been piping melodies of almost saccharine sweetness. It's been hard to avoid the suspicion that there's some sinister sleight of hand at work here, some dark lake troll lurking beneath the innocent rippling waters."

"Certainly many have dredged the lyrics to Hugh Cornwell's mesmeric 'Golden Brown' (incidentally, the group's biggest single success to date) for some concealed meaning, and as for 'Strange Little Girl' — well, would you let your sister tell Jet Black where she was going? Just as Cornwell denies any particular meaning to 'Golden Brown' ('just a few words strung together'), both he and Burnel deny any cold-blooded calculation in the shift of Stranglers' music from the icy grip of *Black And White* to the tuneful ease of their recent hits. They see it as part of continuing evolution. 'The last four or five singles haven't sounded like The Stranglers, according to most people,' says Burnel. 'They think there has to be one sound, but we've always changed'."

"Now with a back catalogue of some seven LPs — most of them chart successes — and a fair litany of hit singles, The Stranglers are on one level one of the most unlikely long-term survivors of the late-seventies upsurge. They started older, already into their maturity, and with a music that was cited as having more in common with The Doors' sixties expeditions than the Nouvelle Vague of the time... In fact, the mainstream rock traditions of most of their output have helped maintain The Stranglers' momentum and appeal — never really in fashion, and therefore never really out of fashion either. No one talks much of The Doors connection these days, long since displaced by the group's later musical wanderings, but the acoustic leanings of 'Cruel Garden' and 'Strange Little Girl' may well have been inspired by a re-examination of another

West Coast sixties phenomenon, Love — or at least, as much is intimated to me by their publicist."

Whilst some fans who had supported The Stranglers since their early days may have been disappointed in the band's change of musical direction, it was something that they would just have to accept. When asked whether The Stranglers would be making any more songs that were more in the vein of '5 Minutes' and 'Hanging Around', Cornwell told BBC radio in January 1983; "I think the feel of the music over the last year or so, it's been a reaction to what we see around us. We're living in an age where technology is getting heavier and heavier. And it's all directed towards communication, increasing communication efficiency, and it's ended up getting to such a state of fine art that people aren't communicating anymore and they have to pick up a phone and speak to each other when they live in like two offices, about three feet apart, with a wall in between and have to speak to each other on the phone. They can't interact as people anymore. And I think this is showing in a lot of the music that's being made now. And so from where I see, our music is getting back to communication."

In response to a fan letter complaining about how 'Golden Brown' was such a strong deviation from the musical stylings of '5 Minutes', Cornwell explained in the same interview; "We're people and we're not machines. Our personalities develop and music is a product of our personality so music must change as well. If he is really into '5 Minutes' I suggest he tries to keep buying new copies of it and keep playing it. With all respect, if your musical taste hasn't developed at all since you heard '5 Minutes' then good luck, really. I'd hate to be standing still or static."

When asked whether The Stranglers were making a deliberate attempt to come up with a more commercial sound, Cornwell said in 1982; "No. We never stand still. We're always developing and the more you use the tools of the trade, you're just getting better and better at it. You're just developing finer and finer styles and it just happens."

On balance, maybe for The Stranglers, reaching commercial success beyond what they had already didn't feel like the be all and end all. Just a few years after the success of *La Folie*, Cornwell told *Smash Hits* in October 1984; "We don't bother whether we're in favour or out of favour. It makes no difference either way." (Burnel told *New Musical Express* in September 1982; "We never considered ourselves really part of what was going on, nor out of it.")

It's understandable as to why there may have been no desire to compete aggressively for chart positions. Offering his opinion on the chart music of the day, Cornwell told *Smash Hits*; "People are attending more to the glamour of it than to the content. They're forgetting what they originally used synthesisers for — which was to complement the song. The song is becoming the reason for the synthesisers in the same way as the video is becoming the excuse for the song."

It comes across that throughout their career, the hypocrisy and fickle nature of the music industry is something that The Stranglers always kept in mind. In particular, in terms of how people were willing to give the band more attention when they had a hit with 'Golden Brown', Cornwell said in 1990; "I think that what happens is the public decides. At a certain point they say, 'Oh, right. Now what's the date today? Okay, right from now on, The Stranglers are going to be a serious thinking man's band.' Actually, I don't know who it is — the press or suddenly the whole mood. That's why fashion happens; things that have been there all the time. But suddenly, this week we're all gonna look at this. Everyone wants to ring you up and wants you to do things. And the thing is, you've been doing exactly the same thing for the last five years and five years ago, they didn't. They couldn't see you."

He said in 2017; "It wasn't just punks who liked it, your

grandmothers liked it. What was nice about it is that it's very subversive, because one of the things it's about is about heroin. It's very nice to hear this song about heroin on the most popular show on radio, with family entertainment. In a way it was more punk than anything else we've done."

If The Stranglers had fallen into the trap of feeling that they had to make music simply to appease the tastes of others, the odds on them continuing may have been much lower. Cornwell told BBC Radio in January 1983; "Everything we do is personal. It's all down to our personal feelings. Otherwise we wouldn't get any joy from doing it."

When asked his thoughts on why The Stranglers had managed to keep going for so long, he said in 1984; "I wouldn't attempt to. It's like asking Salvador Dali why he's the greatest living artist; he wouldn't be able to tell you. All I can say is, in the present lacklustre musical climate, the return of The Stranglers is like a nice, refreshing gust of bad breath."

In 1982, The Stranglers considered that, in terms of being able to work well together, moral was good within the band and functioned as a key factor behind their longevity. "A lot of bands start off as mates at school," said Cornwell. "Then the egos start coming out and they find they're not such mates after all. With us it was the other way round — we didn't know each other at all when we started playing and then we became friends."

Of course, no rapport is perfect and sometimes this had an impact on artistic outcomes. This was the case on *La Folie*. Burnel told *Black & White* in 1982; "Everyone is there for the mixing. Sometimes they want no bass whatsoever or it's me who wants just a little. It essentially depends on the song itself, sometimes even on moods. If, for instance, I have an argument with Hugh, I want lots of bass guitar right in front."

On the frequency and nature of in-band arguments, Burnel said; "Very rarely, but it happens, especially on tour.

I've sometimes even had a few punches at Hugh. He sulks for a few days. I give him a few presents like sending boxes of chocolates through the hotel management. With a little love letter: 'Forgive me, forgive me!'."

On the band's dynamic at the time of making *La Folie*, Burnel said in the same interview; "Jet Black is the integral force of The Stranglers. The stability, the anchor. But he is also the sleeping lion, the sleeping dragon. Once he's angry, he carries the whole world away with him. I've seen him angry a few times. He breaks everything and nothing can stop him. I wouldn't even try myself. There are things going on in his mind... He is a member of a British cult, Exegesis, which means "knowing everything". They destroy the personality in order to rebuild it. A sort of Scientology. There are things I respect in him completely. Dave is very strange. All The Stranglers are strange apart from me. He's a machine, a computer just like Spock in *Star Trek*, completely logical. If you ask him the time, he will tell you the second. In fact no one knows him too well, not even his wife! Hugh is the debonair, wicked intellectual one. He is very cynical and has a very acerbic sense of humour. A humour which is more than black. He never spares anyone and always wants to have the best of everything — the best food, best clothes, best tastes; more than a perfectionist... I believe we are the only group in the world who are straight. The only ones remaining honest to ourselves, artistically speaking and in other ways. We don't lower our sights, we keep the same perspective we had at the beginning. Of course, the way you see things sometimes changes and particularly the way you interpret what you see. But your spiritual purity, that doesn't need to change. Even as you get older."

With Cornwell having left The Stranglers in 1990, in 1995, Black, Burnel and Greenfield made an appearance on Rory Bremner's Christmas special. Together they performed a parody song about politician Gordon Brown (who was Shadow

Chancellor of the Exchequer at the time) to the tune of 'Golden Brown'.

'Golden Brown' has since been covered by hip hop group Kaleef in 1996. Their version got to number twenty-two in the UK. The following year, soul singer Omar did a cover of the song and that got to number thirty-seven.

In a BBC Radio Two listener poll carried out in 2012, 'Golden Brown' was celebrated amongst a list of other great songs that peaked at number two. Other songs in the list included Ultravox's 'Vienna', 'Fairytale Of New York' by The Pogues and Kirsty MacColl, and the Beatles' 'Penny Lane'/'Strawberry Fields Forever'.

Across even more stylistic (and indeed, line-up) changes, The Stranglers would go on to have continued commercial success. Whether or not *La Folie* set them up for this is understandably subject to opinion and debate but really, considering the way in which the album features what was a vital hit single for the band alongside an abundance of memorable and enjoyable songs, there really is nothing quite like it and that is certainly something to be admired and celebrated.

In comparison to the difficulties of 1980 and the earlier part of 1981, it could be said that for The Stranglers, *La Folie* was the album that got them back on track — both commercially and in terms of their morale. It could even be said that *La Folie* was their saving grace; the masterpiece that would put them on the musical map of the eighties and encourage listeners to see them as relevant and excellent musicians. It was a far cry from the press they had received in the late-seventies and it was certainly a positive move compared to what had been some very turbulent years for them.

As one journalist put it in *International Musician & Recording World* in November 1982; "It seems as though The Stranglers are geared up to make their presence felt in the eighties as they did in the latter part of the seventies. Hopefully we are due for a lot more surprises from the Meninblack and the enigmatic foursome have never failed in that capacity yet. After all, when you take a leap in the dark, the last thing you encounter is the predictable."

Discography

Personnel

The Stranglers
Hugh Cornwell – guitar, lead and backing vocals
Jean-Jacques Burnel – bass, backing and lead vocals
Dave Greenfield – keyboards, backing vocals
Jet Black – drums, percussion

Technical
Steve Churchyard – engineer
Tony Visconti – mixing
Jay Pee – art direction
The Stranglers – cover concept
Phil Jude – front cover photography

Track Listing

All lyrics are written by The Stranglers (Hugh Cornwell, Jean-Jacques Burnel, Dave Greenfield and Jet Black), except 'Ain't Nothin' To It', by Milton "Mezz" Mezzrow; all music is composed by The Stranglers.

Side One
1. Non Stop (2:29)
2. Everybody Loves You When You're Dead (2:41)
3. Tramp (3:04)
4. Let Me Introduce You To The Family (3:07)
5. Ain't Nothin' To It (3:56)
6. The Man They Love To Hate (4:22)

Side Two
7. Pin Up (2:46)
8. It Only Takes Two To Tango (3:37)
9. Golden Brown (3:28)
10. How To Find True Love And Happiness In The Present Day (3:04)
11. La Folie (6:04)

2001 CD Reissue Bonus Tracks
12. Cruel Garden (2:14)
13. Cocktail Nubiles (7:08)
14. Vietnamerica (4:01)
15. Love 30 (3:55)
16. You Hold The Key To My Love In Your Hands (2:40)
17. Strange Little Girl (2:40)

2LP self-release additional tracks

Side One (La Folie Extra Texture)
The Man They Love To Hate
Strange Little Girl
Cruel Garden
Love 30
La Folie (Single Edit)
You Hold The Key To My Love In Your Hands

Above tracks taken from the session recorded in London for BBC Radio One on 24th January 1982.

Side Two (Live At Hammersmith Odeon)
Non Stop
The Man They Love To Hate
Golden Brown
How To Find True Love And Happiness In The Present Day
Let Me Introduce You To The Family
Tramp

Above tracks taken from Hammersmith Odeon, London 8th February 1982.

Original releases
LibertyLBG 30342, LP
LibertyTC-LBG 30342, cassette

Reissues:
Fame, EMI FA 4130831, LP, 1984
Fame, Liberty TC-FA 41 3083 4, cassette, 1984
EMI CDP 7 46614 2, CD, 1987
EMI 7243 5 34688 2 8, CD, 2001 (with bonus tracks)
The Stranglers self-release, CGLP, UK 13th April 2018 (2LP)

Other related releases:

In Concert-276

Side One
Down In The Sewer (8:00)
Just Like Nothin On Earth (3:20)
Second Coming (4:13)
Non Stop (2:27)
The Man They Love To Hate (4:45)
Who Wants The World? (2:55)

Side Two
Golden Brown (3:40)
How To Find True Love And Happiness In The Present Day (4:05)
Duchess (2:20)
Let Me Introduce You To The Family (3:05)
Tramp (2:55)
Raven (5:15)
Genetix (5:15)

P = POP/ROCK   31.87

In Concert

No. 276

featuring

the strangters

60'00"

Stereo/Mono
Green Label

The Stranglers are one of Britain's most original and, at the same time, most controversial rock bands. They were among the first of the new-wave outfits to emerge in the mid-'70s and one of the few to survive. The fact that they have survived is a credit to their music and the loyalty of their fans, rather than the pop press who have consistently portrayed them as the villains of the rock scene.

The Stranglers formed in 1974, a couple of years before the punk rock revolution in British music. Their career has run parallel to the punk movement rather than having been a part of it, and their rejection of the punk label has made for an uneasy relationship with a music business which can't cope with a band it can't categorise. Much of The Stranglers' music has been misunderstood; they have often delved into serious subjects in such a tongue-in-cheek way that they have confused their critics.

Since 1977 The Stranglers have released seven albums. With one exception, a live album released in 1979, the albums have been based on a concept or theme. Every album has been, to say the least, provocative and the cause of much critical comment. Much of the criticism has been prompted by intellectual snobbery - what authority does a rock band have to write songs on such matters as genetics, extraterrestrial life, UFOs and nuclear devices? The fact that, between them, the members of The Stranglers have more degrees than the average thermometer seems to have escaped critical attention. Moreover, some of their songs are quite simply good popular music.

The latest Stranglers' album, *La Folie*, is proving their biggest seller to date and a single from it, *Golden Brown*, recently made the top of the U.K. charts. The band claim it's an album of love songs but, as the title suggests, it could only be The Stranglers' view of love.

This IN CONCERT performance includes songs from the three most recent albums, *The Raven*, *The Men In Black* and *La Folie*. The show was recorded at London's Hammersmith Odeon where The Stranglers gave a performance which even their most ardent critics had to admit was superb.

Hugh Cornwell	·	vocals and guitar
Dave Greenfield	·	keyboards
Jean Jacques Burnel	·	bass
Jet Black	·	drums

for programme details see over . . .

CN 03977/S   Issued Wk 19/82
ONE DISK
Rights: Worldwide

TS

BBC Transcription Services CN 3977/S, UK, 10th May 1982
BBC transcription LP for radio broadcasting purposes of show recorded on 8th February 1982 at the Hammersmith Odeon.

Live At The Hammersmith Odeon '81
EMI 7243 4 97773 2 3, CD, UK, 1998
Commercial release of the BBC transcription record. This concert was actually recorded on 8th February 1982. However the original release listed it as Live... 81. It was later reissued with corrected artwork.

Singles
Let Me Introduce You To The Family / Vietnamerica
Liberty UK BP 405, 30th October 1981

Golden Brown / Love 30
Liberty UK BP 407, 1st January 1982

La Folie / Waltzinblack
Liberty UK BP 410, 9th April 1982

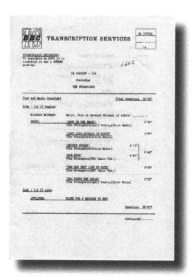

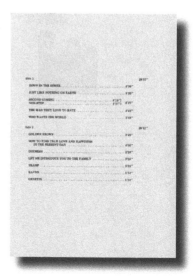

Tour Dates

1981

11th November	The Granary, Bristol
14th November	Norwich University
15th November	Birmingham Odeon
16th November	Sophia Gardens, Cardiff
17th November	Hammersmith Palais
19th November	Southampton Gaumont
20th November	Nottingham Rock City
22nd November	Edinburgh Playhouse
23rd November	Glasgow
24th November	Newcastle City Hall
25th November	Manchester Apollo
26th November	Liverpool Royal Court
27th November	St George's Hall, Bradford
28th November	Sheffield Lyceum
30th November	Ulster Hall, Belfast
2nd December	Loughborough University
3rd December	Bath Pavilion
4th December	Rainbow Theatre, London

1982

21st January	Sheffield Polytechnic
22nd January	Aberystwyth University
23rd January	Leicester University
25th January	Brighton Top Rank
26th January	Guildford Civic Hall
27th January	St Austell Coliseum, Cornwall
28th January	Hemel Hempstead Pavilion
29th January	Victoria Hotel, Hanley
30th January	Swindon Oasis
31st January	Poole Arts Centre
1st February	Bristol Locarno
3rd February	Derby Assembly Rooms
4th February	Warwick University
5th February	Ipswich Gaumont
6th February	Portsmouth Guildhall
7th February	Tiffany's, Leeds
8th February	Hammersmith Odeon, London
9th April	No Nukes Festival, Utrecht, Holland (Broadcast on Dutch TV)
7th August	Vilar de Mouros Festival, Portugal
18th October	TVS Theatre, Gillingham (Broadcast on ITV's *Off The Record*)

In-depth Series

The In-depth series was launched in March 2021 with four titles. Each book takes an in-depth look at an album; the history behind it; the story about its creation; the songs, as well as detailed discographies listing release variations around the world. The series will tackle albums that are considered to be classics amongst the fan bases, as well as some albums deemed to be "difficult" or controversial; shining new light on them, following reappraisal by the authors.

Titles to date:

Jethro Tull - Thick As A Brick	978-1-912782-57-4
Tears For Fears - The Hurting	978-1-912782-58-1
Kate Bush - The Kick Inside	978-1-912782-59-8
Deep Purple - Stormbringer	978-1-912782-60-4
Emerson Lake & Palmer - Pictures At An Exhibition	978-1-912782-67-3
Korn - Follow The Leader	978-1-912782-68-0
Elvis Costello - This Year's Model	978-1-912782-69-7
Kate Bush - The Dreaming	978-1-912782-70-3
Jethro Tull - Minstrel In The Gallery	978-1-912782-81-9
Deep Purple - Fireball	978-1-912782-82-6
Deep Purple - Slaves And Masters	978-1-912782-83-3
Rainbow - Straight Between The Eyes	978-1-912782-96-3
Jethro Tull - Heavy Horses	978-1-912782-97-0
Talking Heads - Remain In Light	978-1-915246-01-1
The Stranglers - La Folie	978-1-915246-02-8
David Bowie - The Rise And Fall Of Ziggy Stardust And The Spiders From Mars	978-1-912782-92-5

CPSIA information can be obtained
at www.ICGtesting.com
Printed in the USA
BVHW022138130522
636961BV00016B/331